Enter These Gates

ALSO BY ALDEN SOLOVY

These Words: Poetic Midrash on the Language of Torah
This Precious Life: Encountering the Divine with Poetry and Prayer
This Joyous Soul: A New Voice for Ancient Yearnings
This Grateful Heart: Psalms and Prayers for a New Day
Jewish Prayers of Hope and Healing
Haggadah Companion: Meditations and Readings

Enter These Gates

Meditations for the Days of Awe

ALDEN SOLOVY

Foreword by Rabbi Naamah Kelman

CCAR
Press

Reform Judaism Publishing, a division of CCAR Press
CENTRAL CONFERENCE OF AMERICAN RABBIS
5784 · NEW YORK · 2024

Published by Reform Judaism Publishing, a division of CCAR Press
Central Conference of American Rabbis
355 Lexington Avenue, New York, NY 10017
(212) 972-3636 | info@ccarpress.org | www.ccarpress.org
Cover art: *Heavens Gateway* © 2024 www.yoramraanan.com

Library of Congress Control Number: 2024937068
ISBN 978-0-88123-651-4 (paperback)
ISBN 978-0-88123652-1 (ebook)

Interior book design and typography by Scott-Martin Kosofsky
    at the Philidor Company, Rhinebeck, NY. www.philidor.com.
Cover design by Barbara Leff.

FSC
www.fsc.org
MIX
Paper from
responsible sources
FSC® C000000

Printed in the U.S.A.
10 9 8 7 6 5 4 3 2 1

For the dead, the wounded, the hostages who live and the hostages who did not survive, for all who were lost—and all that was lost—on October 7, 2023.
For Israel. For the Jewish people.
May wholeness and healing come and everlasting peace.

Contents

Foreword   xiii
Rabbi Naamah Kelman
Acknowledgments   xvii
Introduction   xxi

BLESSING THE NEW YEAR
  Pervasive Peace   2
  Wildly Unimaginable Blessings   3
  Meditation on the Eve of a New Year   5
  Sweet Cake   6
  A New Year Begins   7
  In This Turning: A New Year's Day Meditation   9

CREATION
  Creation Sings   13
  A Moment of Blessing   15
  Time Is the Gift   16
  In Plain Sight   18
  Kneel and Rise   19
  Hidden and Blessed   20

THE BOOKS OF LIFE
  The Book of the Wicked   23
  The Book of the Righteous   24
  The Book of the Between   25
  The Book of Forgiving   26
  The Book of Living   27
  The Archives of Heaven   28

SEEKING HOLINESS
    Of Psalm 27   33
    Hunger for God   35
    Draw Me Close   36
    On the Journey to You   37
    Who Knocks?   39
    When I Pray   41
    Enter These Days   42

VOWS AND COMMITMENTS
    These Vows   45
    All Mitzvot: A *Kol Nidrei* Meditation   47
    Prayer for My Congregation   48
    I Walked with God   49
    Hints of God   50
    The Path to God   51

SHOFAR BLASTS/*SHOFAROT*
    Let Your Heart Stir   55
    The Sound of Holiness   56
    The Path of Righteousness   57
    Clear a Road   59
    Without a Sound   60
    An Hour of Compassion   61

SOVEREIGNTY/*MALCHUYOT*
    God's Plan: An Introspection   65
    Distances   67
    Eternity   68
    Foundation and Sky   69
    Let Prayers Rise   70
    To Be Remembered by God   71
    Crown   73

SIN AND REGRET

    An Easy Sin   77
    Fear   78
    Doubt   79
    Anger   80
    Shame   81
    Allow Your Heart to Break   82
    Sin Offering   83

CONFESSION/*VIDUI*

    Meditation Before *Vidui*   87
    Not Ready   89
    Guilt That Isn't Mine   90
    Am I Ready?   91
    Failures of Joy   92
    Forgiveness Inside   93

REPENTANCE/*T'SHUVAH*

    Repentance Inside   97
    Regarding Old Wounds   99
    Who, Still Broken   101
    My Repentance   104
    Join Me   105
    Cry No More   107
    The Silence That Speaks   108
    Small and Large   109

FORGIVENESS/*S'LICHAH*

    Remembering My Humanity   113
    To Be Free   114
    When the Light Doesn't Shine   115
    Forgiving God   116
    Opposites and Antidotes   118

The High Priest   119
Why Forgive   121
Forgiving the Unforgivable   122

THE ANCIENT JOURNEY
Village   127
Artifact   128
Winepress   129
These Ancient Stones   131
Seeking God   132
Ancient Dawn   133
History   134

FRAILTY
Walking Toward Sunset   137
Look for Me   138
Unfinished Business   139
To Relieve Fear   140
God Arrives   141
On the Day of My Death   143
My Rock   144

JUSTICE
Is This the Fast?   147
Why Do You Slumber?   149
What to Cherish   151
Humble Before God   152
Strive   153
Where Is Mercy?   154

MEMORY/YIZKOR
On Lighting a Memorial Candle   157
For the Bereaved   158

Mourner's Lament   159
For Bereaved Children   160
Shoah Memorial Prayer   161
O Auschwitz, O Birkenau   162
Eileh Ezk'rah After October 7   163

AT THE GATES/*N'ILAH*
The Entry to Our Hearts   166
Keep the Gates Open   167
Unlock the Gates   168
At the Gates   170
Meditation Before *N'ilah*   172
Your Gate   174

Permissions   175
Index of Liturgical Uses   177
Index of Hebrew References   183
About the Author   185

Foreword

Rabbi Naamah Kelman

THE DAYS OF AWE always seem to come upon us too early, even when they are later in the Gregorian calendar. Somehow, we are never prepared. And as I write this in the latter half of 5784, I suspect that the coming year will be different and more challenging than before. Just days after we welcomed the new year, a terrible war broke out. Many are calling October 7 *Shabbat HaSh'chorah*, the Sabbath of Darkness. The root of darkness in Hebrew is ש-ח-ר, *shin-chet-reish*; this same root gives us the words *shachar* (dawn) and *Shacharit* (Morning Service). The High Holy Days are exactly that "new dawn" that emerges from the past, and sometimes from darkness. Alden Solovy's *Enter These Gates* is the very invitation we need to restart and enter the new year. His words, written before and after October 7, somehow manage to shine a bright light into our spirits and offer a beacon of hope to all of us, regardless of what we may be going through. He is our guide from darkness to light, knowing wisely that we often need support to get there.

I have often wondered why Yom Kippur comes after Rosh HaShanah. Wouldn't it make more sense if it were the opposite? To first cleanse ourselves, start with contrition, reflection, atonement, and then greet the new year? Yet our liturgical heritage has us first celebrating the Creation, the renewal of God's majesty, and then we face God's judgment. We begin the new year with promise and hope and then spend the intermediate days seeking forgiveness from our fellows, culminating with Yom Kippur when we stand as a collective reciting our sins and praying for mercy. Rosh HaShanah is a reminder that we can experience God—and God's love and compassion—filled with wonder and gratitude, preparing us for life's losses and struggles. Perhaps we need that reminder so we can be better prepared for the solemnity and seriousness of Yom Kippur. We first need to experience through the liturgy and the Biblical passages, the wonders of God—specifically God's relationship to us.

Most of our prayers are recited with our collective voice. There is strength in this collective framing; however, the individual yearning for God's presence can get lost. Abraham, Sarah, Hagar, Isaac, Hannah, and Jonah—Biblical figures that feature in the High Holy Day Torah and Haftarah readings—interact directly with a God who shows compassion and forgiveness. Similarly, Alden Solovy's prayer poems give each and every one of us a language for seeking after and hoping for a direct and intimate experience of God. His pieces powerfully resonate with the traditional prayers but make space for us as individuals. Our prayers and scriptures are in Hebrew, with all the layers of meaning they hold; Solovy writes in English. In doing so, he gives the praying, meditating person the rhythms and sounds of our traditional prayers. Those familiar with the Hebrew can listen for the original, and those who are not will get a strong sense of the nature and flow of Jewish prayer for the High Holy Days.

Our people's worship is rooted from Biblical times in offering sacrifices; with the destruction of the Temples in Jerusalem, we turned to words of prayer, study, and acts of lovingkindness to replace the ancient rituals. For centuries we have relied on words. More recently, we have incorporated traditions of meditation, silence, *nigunim* (wordless melodies), and *hitbod'dut* (solitary prayer in nature). The fact that these prayer poems are designed with so much white space on each page leaves room for these other practices. One can read to oneself, then pause to meditate or sing a *nigun*, or go out for a walk while repeating some of Solovy's guiding words through mindfulness exercises. Solovy's texts can also serve as a basis for study and discussion in small groups, in *chavruta*. However it is used, this collection is a source book for deepening one's prayer life.

One of the special blessings of living in Jerusalem—and all of Israel, for that matter—is the unique experience of Yom Kippur. Israel's Jewish citizens almost completely shut down their daily activities, and a mysterious quiet fills the streets. In Jerusalem especially, many Jews wear white, and besides bicycles, most traffic stops. One can almost imagine the centuries past, when the hills of Jerusalem were surrounded by wilderness. If you are standing in the right place, you can draw a line from the ancient Temple, out of one of the ancient city's gates. From there, the scapegoat carrying our sins was taken to the Judean Hills. We Reform Jews no longer pray for the rebuilding of the Temple nor the restoration of the priestly class and the sacrifices brought. So how might one create this Jerusalem experience, feeling the sense of the Holy, listening to the silence, hearing the cries, and wiping away the tears of joy to start a new year? How do we experience the hills and valleys of our lives and renew and heal ourselves and others? Alden Solovy's *Enter These Gates: Meditations for the Days of Awe* shows us the way.

RABBI NAAMAH KELMAN *served as Dean of Hebrew Union College–Jewish Institute of Religion in Jerusalem from 2008 to 2023, where she was ordained as the first woman rabbi in Israel. She served in various positions there and remains an activist for feminism, pluralism, and peace.*

Acknowledgments

FOR MONTHS after October 7, I cried. I cried at the drop of a hat. I cried and cried and cried. On that day, this book was about 90 percent completed, but I did not feel capable of finishing it. Worse, I lost faith in what I had already written. All of my writing energy was ripped away from this text and forced by a will of its own into war poetry. I couldn't imagine writing anything other than war poetry. I told the publishers that I would not finish the manuscript. "Not so fast," they said. "Send us what you've got. We'll be the judge of that."

It was not the first time I told them that I was walking away from writing poetry inspired by Torah and *t'filah* (prayer). After writing *These Words: Poetic Midrash on the Language of Torah*, I told leaders at CCAR Press that I had written my last book. I was convinced that *These Words* took every single drop of creativity out of me. "Not so fast," they said. "We have this idea for a book for the High Holy Days, and it's got your name on it."

And so, I begin these acknowledgments with the Central Conference of American Rabbis, *b'gadol* (at large). The CCAR—and its CCAR Press—have been generous to me in more ways than I can count. Believing in me when I didn't believe in myself is perhaps the greatest gift of all.

Thank you to Cantor Erin Miles Frankel and Rodeph Shalom, Philadelphia, for commissioning "Creation Sings" as lyrics for a new High Holy Day liturgical song, as well as the support of the congregation's Lee Stanley Music Fund.

Thanks to Cantor Frankel and AJ Luca for the beautiful music that they wrote for these lyrics. Cantorial soloist Rebecca Schwartz composed compelling music for "Pervasive Peace." "Keep the Gates Open" was commissioned by Rabbi Andrea London for a High Holy Day greeting card from Beth Emet–The Free Synagogue. "Why Do You Slumber?" was inspired by teachings of Tovah Leah Nachmani of the Pardes Institute of Jewish Studies. "Clear a Road" was inspired by Pardes's Jamie Salter as he guided in the south of Israel. "At the Gates" was inspired by a song written by my cousin Rabbi Irwin Keller. "These Ancient Stones" came out of a CCAR rabbinic mission to Israel, at which I led a writing session. Thanks to you all.

My writing is carried by the love and support of my family and friends. To my mother and sisters, thank you for your love and encouragement. To my daughters, Nikki and Dana, both writers who have come into their own powerful voices, I cherish our conversations about writing, writers, and books. Your support and enthusiasm for my work mean more to me than I can express.

I am honored that Rabbi Donald Goor, chair of the CCAR Press Council, continues to advocate for my work, as he has since the beginning of my relationship with CCAR. Thanks to the entire CCAR Press Council for supporting this project.

Many thanks to my friend and Jerusalem neighbor Rabbi Naamah Kelman for her insightful foreword, which elevates issues core to writing this book. I am honored by her kind words about my poetry. It is a delight to share the cover with her.

Throughout the years, the CCAR Press professional team have steadfastly supported our projects. Thank you, Deborah Smilow and Chiara Ricisak. Special thanks to

Raquel Fairweather-Gallie for your continued enthusiasm, passionate professionalism, and ongoing efforts in marketing and promoting all our collaborations.

Thanks to copyeditor Debra Hirsch Corman, who has applied her skills to each of my CCAR Press volumes, showing a deep love and care for my work, as well as an understanding of my voice and a commitment to its integrity. Thanks also to Michelle Kwitkin for proofreading and Scott-Martin Kosofsky for designing, each of whom also worked their magic on my previous books.

As with my other four CCAR Press volumes, this book began with a conversation with Rabbi Hara Person, CCAR's chief executive, followed by one with CCAR Press director Rafael Chaiken. When I said I was done writing liturgical work, it was Hara and Rafael who refused to allow it. When I told Rafael and editor Rabbi Anne Villarreal-Belford that I would not complete the manuscript, they refused to allow it. Annie took the not-quite-completed manuscript—the one for which I'd lost faith—read it, commented on it in so many loving and important ways, and showed me the beauty and value in my own work. There are no words of thanks that can adequately reflect the *chesed* and *rachamim* (love and compassion) that Annie gave to me.

My work is also carried by you, my reader. To the clergy and congregants, professionals and laypersons, who have followed, encouraged, purchased, celebrated, and used my work—thank you from the bottom of my heart. You are why I write.

Introduction

ONE DAY, you will walk out into the world and you won't recognize it. Core assumptions that you held about yourself and the universe will call out to be reexamined. Perhaps it will be a personal moment: a birth or a death, a moment of joy or a moment of pain. Perhaps it will be a communal experience.

On October 7, 2023, Atzeret/Simchat Torah, anxiously waiting for another "all clear" in our building's bomb shelter in Jerusalem, we all knew that our lives in Israel—and around the world—were being shattered. It was supposed to be a day of joy and celebration, the culmination of the High Holy Day season.

If you are blessed to live long enough, the odds are high that you'll experience both the joys and the sorrows that challenge one's way of being.

Rosh HaShanah evening, more than a decade ago. I was in my home congregation in Evanston, Illinois, for the first time since making *aliyah* to Jerusalem. The room was packed, the retractable wall between the sanctuary and social hall opened to make space for the assembly. Sitting in the main sanctuary, about two-thirds of the way back, gave me a broad view of the gathering. As the service began and the assembled settled into the moment, I looked across the crowd toward the ark.

The vision couldn't have lasted more than two or three seconds. Gray-black smoke appeared to rise off of the congregation. The *Sh'ma*, formed in perfect scribal calligraphy with the crowns and flourishes, stretched upward from the assembled—upward, upward—connecting the congregation with realms above. In that instant, heaven connected to earth. I blinked. The vision of Torah script in wisps of smoke was gone.

Yom Kippur morning, a few years earlier. I walked into that same sanctuary through a side door opening into a no-man's land aisle between the formal sanctuary and the social hall, the tracks of the now stowed retractable wall visible on the floor. My hope that morning was to avoid seeing anyone I knew, assuming my friends would be seated more toward the front of the congregation. Walking in, I made almost immediate eye contact with a friend from Shabbat morning services. When our eyes met, I began to cry. He is among the few who know what I am about to share.

My wife Ami *z"l* attempted suicide several times. Each attempt was dramatic and difficult. That year, on Rosh HaShanah, Ami attempted suicide by fire. Fortunately, she poured the gasoline around her feet, rather than onto herself. By the grace of God and swift action by police, she survived that attempt with minimal physical injuries. When I walked into services that Yom Kippur, she was safely held in a locked psychological unit. The words of Yom Kippur liturgy echoed through my heart that day . . . Who by fire, indeed.

What a strange thing we do each year at the High Holy Days: We put our own humanity on trial. We take an accounting of our souls precisely at the moment we celebrate the creation of the world and lift up the sovereignty of God. We take accounting of our own souls because the world needs us each at our best, because part of perfecting God's world is healing ourselves. Even though we know that the world will offer us moments of challenge—like September 11 and October 7—we choose to look deeply at our lives again and again, year after year.

The High Holy Days can lift us on words of Torah and prayer to the heights of our best selves. The days also call forth the deepest moments of our vulnerability and pain. Our memories—joyous and painful—meet our hopes for the future. These are the days of our most intimate self-assessment. By design, our liturgy brings out our sorrows, our fears, and our vulnerabilities. Yet the intent—far from punishment or retribution—is to lift us toward our best selves. Repentance. Prayer. Charity. Confession. Forgiveness. We ask a lot of ourselves and our liturgy. Our liturgy and our tradition ask a lot from us.

Enter These Gates has two purposes. The first is to serve as a source of new meditations for private use, a path to deepening our individual experiences of the Days of Awe. The second is as a new liturgical supplement to *Mishkan HaNefesh: Machzor for the Days of Awe*, which has been in use for more than a decade. Central to this book is the goal of helping clergy and congregations bring refreshed vigor and new voices into High Holy Day worship. *Enter These Gates* can also be used in conjunction with *Mishkan HaLev: Prayers for S'lichot and the Month of Elul*.

This volume offers more than one hundred new readings based on the core thematic elements of the High Holy Day liturgy. Some of the works are traditional in form and language, recognizable as riffs on particular prayers. Other prayer poems offered here blend traditional themes with storytelling, music-like interlude, or liturgical reframing. My hopes are that:

- Rabbis and other clergy incorporate some of this work into High Holy Day worship, including S'lichot and *Tashlich*.

- Congregations place copies of *Enter These Gates* in their pews and prayer bookshelves so that congregants and participants can encounter this work in private prayer during services.
- Individuals use this volume during the month of Elul and the Days of Awe as part of their own personal journeys of High Holy Day preparation.
- Educators use this volume for supplemental prayer in religious school worship in the weeks leading up to the High Holy Days, as well as for teaching High Holy Day themes.
- Rabbis, clergy, and educators use *Enter These Gates* to teach about the High Holy Days in adult education and conversion classes.

This is my second CCAR Press volume written as a supplement to our liturgy. *This Joyous Soul: A New Voice for Ancient Yearnings* offers readings to be used alongside *Mishkan T'filah: A Reform Siddur*. Unlike that book—organized to follow the table of contents in *Mishkan T'filah*—*Enter These Gates* is organized thematically. Some of the connections between the prayer poems in this book and the liturgy in *Mishkan HaNefesh* will be clear simply by the chapter name or the title of the poem. Other connections are less obvious. To assist the reader in matching prayer poems in this volume with the formal liturgy, see the Index of Liturgical Uses. Citations of the biblical and liturgical quotes are listed in the Index of Hebrew References.

One day you will wake, as you have before, and it will be a day, God forbid, like September 11 in the United States or October 7 in Israel. You will walk out into the world and you won't recognize it. Perhaps it will be the day your world shuts down because of a global pandemic. Perhaps you'll have a vision of love from heaven written in sacred letters of Torah. Or maybe there will be a fire in your life here on earth, *chas v'shalom*, heaven forbid. The High Holy Days call out to us to confront life on life's terms and to challenge ourselves to see our frailties and our strengths.

The introduction to *Mishkan HaNefesh* asks, "Opening a prayer book on the High Holy Days, what do we hope to find?" If a *machzor* (High Holy Day prayer book) is successful, it goes on to say, "It leads us on a path across rough terrain." Soul searching. Introspection. Mortality. Our shortcomings. Our beliefs. "It tests our spiritual stamina, and we do well to make use of imagination and memory."

Although *Enter These Gates* is a book of prayers and meditations for the High Holy Days, don't be fooled. It is really a mirror. A dream. A doorway. It is a book of imagination and memory, a book of challenges and warnings, a book of hopes and aspirations. It is a descent into fire and an ascent into secrets that rise to heaven.

Bless you on your journey.

Blessing the New Year

Four days serve as the New Year. The first of
Nisan is the New Year for kings and festivals.
The first of Elul is the New Year for animal
tithes. . . . The first of Tishrei is the New Year
for counting years. . . . The first of Sh'vat
is the New Year for the fruit trees. . . . Beit
Hillel says: The New Year for trees is on the
fifteenth of Sh'vat.

—*Mishnah Rosh HaShanah* 1:1

Pervasive Peace

May it be Your will, God of our fathers and mothers,
That the year ahead brings a pervasive and complete peace
On all the inhabitants of the earth,
Beyond all the dreams of humanity.

יְהִי רָצוֹן מִלְּפָנֶיךָ, אֱלֹהֵי אֲבוֹתֵינוּ וְאִמּוֹתֵינוּ,
שֶׁהַשָּׁנָה הַבָּאָה תָּבִיא שָׁלוֹם מֻחְלָט וְשָׁלֵם
עַל כָּל־יוֹשְׁבֵי תֵבֵל,
מֵעֵבֶר לְכָל־חֲלוֹמוֹת הָאֱנוֹשׁוּת.

Y'hi ratzon mil'fanecha, Elohei avoteinu v'imoteinu,
Shehashanah habaah tavi shalom muchlat v'shaleim
Al kol yosh'vei teiveil,
Mei-eiver l'chol chalomot ha-enoshut.

Wildly Unimaginable Blessings

Let us dream
Wildly unimaginable blessings . . .
Blessings so unexpected,
Blessings so beyond our hopes for this world,
Blessings so unbelievable in this era,
That their very existence
Uplifts our vision of Creation,
Our relationships to each other,
And our yearning for life itself.

Let us dream
Wildly unimaginable blessings . . .
A complete healing of mind, body, and spirit,
A complete healing for all,
The end of suffering and strife,
The end of plague and disease,
When kindness flows from the river of love,
When goodness flows from the river of grace,
Awakened in the spirit of all beings,
When God's light,
Radiating holiness,
Is seen by everyone.

Let us pray—
With all our hearts—
For wildly unimaginable blessings,
So that God will hear the call
To open the gates of the Garden,
Seeing that we haven't waited,
That we've already begun to repair the world,

Each of us becoming a blessing,
In testimony to our faith in life,
Our faith in each other,
And our faith in the Holy One,
The Source of all blessings.

Meditation on the Eve of a New Year

God,
We stand at the cusp of a new year,
Looking forward, looking backward,
So much accomplished,
So much neglected,
Gains and losses,
Joys and sorrows,
Victories and defeats.
A life.
My life.

You,
God of Old,
You are Steadfast Witness,
Source and Shelter.
I bend my heart to You,
Recalling all of Your gifts.

God,
For consolation in my grief,
For sunlight and midnight,
For hope in my celebrations,
For warmth and for shelter,
For current and tide,
For family and for friends,
For the flow of beauty and grace,
I bend my life back to You,
As the New Year descends,
In love and in service,
My offering
To Your holy name.

Sweet Cake

Give me a drop of honey,
And I will give you the harvest moon.
Give me a silent tear,
And I will give you the roaring sea.
Give me a cup of milk,
And I will give you the rising sun.
Give me your secret prayer,
And I will give you my broken heart.

Give me a drop of honey,
And we will make a feast of this life.
Sweet cake,
To feed ourselves with joy and love.
Sweet cake,
To feed the world with awe and wonder.
Sweet cake,
Of milk and honey.
Sweet cake,
Of prayers and tears.

A New Year Begins

Every moment a new year begins.
Something lost.
Something gained.
Every day, a new challenge.
Every hour, a new choice.
Every second, a new chance.

God of Old,
In this moment, a baby will be born,
And a child will die.
In this moment, lovers will marry,
And others will split.
In this moment, someone will hear
That their medical treatments succeeded,
And others will be told
To prepare to die.

Every moment a new year begins.
Something lost.
Something gained.
Let me breathe in a soul of compassion
And breathe out a soul of peace,
Loving gently in the morning
And ferociously at night,
Dancing wildly at dawn
And slowly at dusk,
Crooning full voice at midday,
Singing quietly at midnight.

Creator of all,
Every moment a new year begins.
The flow of fresh light from heaven

Touches our hearts.
Something lost.
Something gained.
Let it be for blessing.
Let it be for healing.
Let it be for shelter.
Let it be for wisdom and strength.
Let us be, in this moment,
Your messengers of kindness on earth.

In This Turning: A New Year's Day Meditation

Darkness and grace
Mourning and thunder
Light and rejoicing
Daybreak and open sky

Here I surrender
To the chance for love
Your warm breath
Your loving hands
The hope in your heart

What gifts await in this turning
To you
To myself
This joy
This adventure

What gifts wait in this turning
And this yearning
This new year
This new wonder

Let blessings rain down
Upon us from heaven
And let hope settle softly
Upon this open heart

Let this be the time to sing
To dance
To play
And to delight in another
Glorious
Day

Creation

Rabbi Eliezer says, "In Tishrei the world was created."

—Babylonian Talmud, *Rosh HaShanah* 10b

Rabbi Sh'muel bar Yitzchak said, "According to whom do we pray, 'Today is the day of the beginning of Your Creation'? According to Rabbi Eliezer, who said that in Tishrei the world was created."

—Babylonian Talmud, *Rosh HaShanah* 27a

Creation Sings

Then the sun rose
For the first time,
To warm the land,
To warm our hearts,
To warm our hands.

Tides shifting,
Birds winging,
Flowers bursting,
Clouds drifting,
Eden singing.

And light sparkled,
The heavens shimmered,
While love echoed,
The future glimmered.

הַיּוֹם הֲרַת עוֹלָם.
הַיּוֹם הֲרַת עוֹלָם.
Hayom harat olam.
Hayom harat olam.
Today is the birthday of the world.
Today is the birthday of our world.

Let the sun rise
On a new day,
To warm the land,
To warm our hearts,
To warm our hands.

Light still sparkles
From Creation,
Love still echoes,
The world's foundation.

הַיּוֹם הֲרַת עוֹלָם.
הַיּוֹם הֲרַת עוֹלָם.
Hayom harat olam.
Hayom harat olam.
Today is the birthday of the world.
Today is the birthday of our world.

So these hours
Of introspection
And these moments
Of deep reflection
Will bring us back
To God's Creation
And lift our hearts
With jubilation.

הַיּוֹם הֲרַת עוֹלָם.
הַיּוֹם הֲרַת עוֹלָם.
Hayom harat olam.
Hayom harat olam.
Today is the birthday of the world.
Today is the birthday of our world.

A Moment of Blessing

Every breath and every blink,
Every moment and every heartbeat:
Each one, a blessing.
This is a moment of blessing.
Blessings given. Blessings received.

Every trail and every vista,
Every journey and every homecoming:
Each one, an adventure.
This is a moment of adventure.
Adventures alone. Adventures together.

Every sunrise and every sunset,
Every crash of thunder and every roar of the sea:
Each one, a moment of majesty.
This is a moment of majesty.
Majesty from heaven. Majesty on earth.

Every birth and every death,
Every love and every loss:
Each one, a mystery.
This is a moment of mystery.
Mysteries hidden. Mysteries revealed.

Blessed are You, Adonai our God,
God of blessings, God of adventures,
God of majesty and God of mystery,
You fill our days with Your glory
And our lives with precious gifts.
Praised are You, Source of love.

Time Is the Gift

This moment has never happened before.
Perhaps it will be just like the one before it.
Perhaps it will be just like the one after it.
And this moment is still ripe with all that might be.

This hour has never happened before.
Perhaps it will be just like the one before it.
Perhaps it will be just like the one after it.
And this hour is still ripe with all that might be.

This day has never happened before.
Perhaps it will be just like the one before it.
Perhaps it will be just like the one after it.
And this day is still ripe with all that might be.

Source of our lives,
Source of our days,
The new year starts in an instant—
A moment, an hour, a day—
Sometimes without being noticed,
So that years can pass in a fog.

Time is the gift
That seems endless,
Until it ends.
Time is the gift
Of each new year,
A reminder that
This day is new.
It has never been before,
And it will never be again.

הַיּוֹם הֲרַת עוֹלָם.

Hayom harat olam.

This is the day that the world came into being.
This is the day that God created the world.
This is the day that we remember
To remember
The minutes, hours, and days of our lives.

In Plain Sight

Ancient One,
God of Old,
Teacher, Guide, and Shelter,
Your gifts are hidden in plain sight.
Why do I struggle to see
Love and light,
Hope and tomorrow,
The moment that just was
And the moment that will be?
This joyous soul?
This grieving heart?
The gifts of this life?

Source of all being,
Grant me the vision to see the gifts around me,
The wisdom to share Your bounty and grace,
And the humility to praise Your holy name.

Kneel and Rise

I bend my knees
To bless the earth,
My hands in mud,
The water soaking into
The legs of my jeans.

I rise to bless the sky,
My muddy hands
Reaching into the vastness,
The warmth
Flowing down my face.

I bless myself with love
And bless you with love
So that together
We can bless each other
And all who live
With love.

Let our blessings be like thunder
And our joy fly free.
Let all who live and breathe
Kneel to bless and rise to bless,
Kneel to be blessed and rise to be blessed,
With the goodness and the love
That flows through Creation.

Hidden and Blessed

Hidden in soil,
Waiting,
There is a moment
When a seed bursts forth
With new life.

Hidden in a cloud,
Waiting,
There is a moment
When water bursts forth
To feed the land.

Earth and sky.
Seed and rain.
Creation renewed.

Hidden in chaos
There was a moment
When God called light
Out of the darkness
To create all that is
And all that might be.

Bless this day
That summons our ancient memories
Of the first moments
Of beauty and life.

The Books of Life

Three books are open in heaven on Rosh
HaShanah: one of wholly wicked people, one
of wholly righteous people, and one for those
people in between, neither wholly wicked or
wholly good.

—Babylonian Talmud, *Rosh HaShanah* 16b

The Book of the Wicked

When I pick up
The book of the completely wicked
Looking for my own name,
Looking for signs that my sins
Have tarnished my life
Beyond redemption,
My hands become encrusted
With filth,
The remains of evil
That pour forth
From the volume.

Try as I may
To find myself there,
Unredeemable,
My fate unmovable,
Freeing me of the work ahead—
The work of t'shuvah,
Renewal and repair,
The work of t'filah,
Introspection and prayer,
The work of tzedakah,
Charity and care.
My hands,
Unstained by the evil of others,
Are mine to use in service to God,
And my destiny,
Empowered by service,
Remains my choice.

The Book of the Righteous

When I pick up
The book of the completely righteous
Looking for my own name,
Looking for signs that my heart
Shines with the light of goodness,
My hands glow
With the beauty
That pours forth
From the volume.

Try as I may
To find myself there,
Redeemed,
My fate with the *tzaddikim* and *tzaddikot*
Of the generations,
My hands become blessed
By the goodness of others,
By their hopes and their aspirations
For our people,
To do the work of *t'shuvah*,
Renewal and repair,
The work of *t'filah*,
Introspection and prayer,
The work of *tzedakah*,
Charity and care.
My destiny,
Empowered by love,
Remains my choice.

The Book of the Between

When I pick up
The book of the between,
The book of those who are neither
Completely wicked nor completely righteous,
I find my name easily
Among the masses,
For I live,
Sometimes good,
Sometimes not so good,
Making choices
Day by day,
As most of us do.

Our work is clear
But not easy,
The work of *t'shuvah*,
Renewal and repair,
The work of *t'filah*,
Introspection and prayer,
The work of *tzedakah*,
Charity and care.
How I use my hands
And how I shape my destiny
Are my choice
And mine alone.

The Book of Forgiving

Remember and inscribe us
In the book of forgiving:
The book of forgiving ourselves,
The book of forgiving each other,
The book of forgiving our families,
The book of forgiving our friends,
The book of forgiving our faults,
The book of forgiving our weaknesses,
The book of forgiving our mistakes,
The book of forgiving our misdeeds,
The book of forgiving poor choices,
The book of forgiving lost opportunities,
So long as we have breaths in our bodies
And sparks in our souls.

As long as we live
Let us be alive,
In service to our God,
Our people,
And all of humanity.

The Book of Living

Remember and inscribe us
In the book of living:
The book of living in wonder,
The book of living in awe,
The book of living in righteousness,
The book of living Your Torah,
The book of living Your mitzvot,
The book of living *tikkun olam*,
The book of living *tzedakah*,
The book of living each day fully,
The book of living each day faithfully,
The book of living each day for You,
So long as we have breaths in our bodies
And sparks in our souls.

As long as we live
Let us be alive,
In service to our God,
Our people,
And all of humanity.

The Archives of Heaven

How many volumes of blessings
Can there be in the archives of heaven,
Stretching back in time to Creation?

סֵפֶר חַיִּים טוֹבִים
Sefer chayim tovim
The Book of a Good Life

סֵפֶר גְּאֻלָּה וִישׁוּעָה
Sefer g'ulah vishuah
The Book of Redemption and Deliverance

סֵפֶר פַּרְנָסָה וְכַלְכָּלָה
Sefer parnasah v'chalkalah
The Book of Livelihood and Sustenance

סֵפֶר זְכֻיּוֹת
Sefer z'chuyot
The Book of Merits

סֵפֶר סְלִיחָה וּמְחִילָה
Sefer s'lichah umchilah
The Book of Pardon and Forgiveness

How wonderful
To know that the precincts of heaven
Are rich with volume after volume
Cataloging our blessings
And the blessings of our ancestors
Throughout eternity.

Inscribe us, we plead,
In them all.

בְּסֵפֶר חַיִּים, בְּרָכָה, וְשָׁלוֹם, וּפַרְנָסָה טוֹבָה,
נִזָּכֵר וְנִכָּתֵב לְפָנֶיךָ, אֲנַחְנוּ וְכָל עַמְּךָ
בֵּית יִשְׂרָאֵל, לְחַיִּים טוֹבִים וּלְשָׁלוֹם.

*B'sefer chayim, b'rachah, v'shalom, ufarnasah tovah,
nizacheir v'nikateiv l'fanecha—anachnu v'chol am'cha
beit Yisrael—l'chayim tovim ulshalom.*

Let us, and the whole family of Israel, be remembered
and inscribed in the Book of Life. May it be a life of
goodness, blessing, and prosperity! May it be a life of
peace!

Seeking Holiness

What is service of the heart? It is prayer.

—Babylonian Talmud, *Taanit* 2a

Of Psalm 27

One impossible request,
One incredible hope,
One audacious dream,
We pray for
Again and again . . .
To live in God's house
All the days of our lives,
To gaze on God's beauty,
And to dwell in God's palace.

Yearning of yearnings . . .
Mystery of mysteries . . .
Wonder beyond wonders . . .
Can we find the way
Home to holiness?
Can we ascend
The long stairway
To righteousness?
Can we stand
In the holy light
That fills the plaza
Of the heavens?

O, to be worthy of even a moment
In God's presence,
To be graced with a glimpse
Of the sanctuary of the Divine,
And to stand before the Throne of Glory.

אַחַת שָׁאַלְתִּי מֵאֵת־יהוה אוֹתָהּ אֲבַקֵּשׁ:
שִׁבְתִּי בְּבֵית־יהוה כָּל־יְמֵי חַיַּי,
לַחֲזוֹת בְּנֹעַם־יהוה וּלְבַקֵּר בְּהֵיכָלוֹ.

Achat shaalti mei-eit Adonai, otah avakeish:
shivti b'veit Adonai kol y'mei chayai,
lachazot b'no-am Adonai ulvakeir b'heichalo.

One thing I ask of Adonai, the one thing I desire: that I
might dwell in Your house all the days of my life, to behold
Your graciousness, and to enter God's sanctuary.

Hunger for God

The day of judgment has come,
And I hunger for God.
For the God of justice,
The God of righteousness,
The Maker of worlds,
The Sovereign of eternity.

The day of judgment has come,
And I hunger for mercy.
For the mercy I offer you,
And the mercy I offer myself.
For the mercy of God,
And the mercy of humanity.

The day of judgment has come,
The day that wipes away
The fragile boundaries
Between love and fear,
Joy and loss,
Hope and sorrow,
Darkness and light,
To leave a breathless wonder.

The day of judgment has come,
And I hunger for God.
The God of my ancestors,
The God of my history,
The God of my heritage,
The Sovereign of eternity.

Draw Me Close

Draw me close to You,
God of life,
That I might live
In Your glory
And in Your holiness.

Draw me close to You,
God of joy,
That I might rejoice
In Your glory
And in Your holiness.

Draw me close to You,
God of mystery,
That I might marvel
In Your glory
And in Your holiness.

On the Journey to You

On the journey to You
I stumble and fall.
I bring my broken heart
And injured soul
Looking for healing
And love.

Let me see
Your radiance and Your splendor,
Your heart and Your hope.

There is no journey
Without You.
There is no wilderness
And no sky
Without You.
There is no me
Without You.

Let me see
Your radiance and Your splendor,
Your heart and Your hope.

This is my prayer for my prayers,
My hope for my hopes,
My dream for my dreams,
The love I have for You
And all of Creation.

On the journey to You
I stumble and fall.
You heal my broken heart
And injured soul
With compassion,
With grace,
And with love.

Who Knocks?

Who knocks
At the doorway of my heart?

Perhaps it is God asking:
Have you loved Me
With all of your heart,
All of your soul,
And all of your being?

Perhaps it is the Jewish people asking:
Have you stood by us,
Supported us,
Endowed us with wisdom,
Building institutions of Torah and prayer?

Perhaps it is generations past asking:
Have you honored us,
Celebrated us,
Telling our stories
And cherishing our memory?

Perhaps it is generations future asking:
Have you transmitted this legacy,
Teaching the love of God,
Devotion to Torah,
And the beauty of mitzvot?

Perhaps it is we asking:
Have we been true to all we believe,
All that we value,
All that we hold dear?

Who knocks
At the doorway of my heart?
Awe. Beauty. Compassion. Devotion.
Endurance. Forgiveness. Gratitude.
Humility. Inspiration. Joy. Kindness.
Love. Mercy. Nobility. Optimism.
Patience. Quiet. Righteousness.
Serenity. Trust. Understanding.
Vision. Willingness. Yearning. Zeal.

Stand with me at the doorway of my heart,
And I will stand with you at the doorway of yours.
We will sing and pray
Together with all who seek Torah,
All who practice mitzvot,
All who pledge our lives in service
To God's holy name.

When I Pray

When I pray
With a heart of repentance,
Holiness enters,
Bringing *Shechinah*
To bless the moment
With beauty and grace.

When I pray
With a heart of forgiveness,
Radiance enters,
Bringing *Ein Sof*
To bless the moment
With awe and wonder.

When I pray
With a heart of faith,
Love enters,
Bringing *HaMakom*
To bless the moment
With renewal and light.

When I pray
With a heart of truth,
Mercy enters,
Bringing *Rachmana*
To bless the moment
With joy and salvation.

Let my prayers rise up
To You, *El Elyon*, and
Let blessings rain
Down on all the earth.

Enter These Days

Enter
These days of awe
As a pilgrim
On a journey
To hear
The voice of God
That echoes from
Within.

Enter
These days of awe
As a seeker
On a mission
To discover
The voice of God
That echoes from
Beyond.

Enter
These days of awe
As an adventurer
On a quest
To reach the secret place
Where the voice of God
Within
Sings blessings
In harmony
With the voice of God from
Beyond.

Vows and Commitments

It is better that you should not vow than that you should vow and not pay.

—Ecclesiastes 5:4

With regard to that verse, Rabbi Meir said, "Better than the one who vows and does not pay, and the one who vows and pays, is one who does not take a vow at all."

—Babylonian Talmud, *Chulin* 2a

These Vows

You have been summoned
To wander,
In search of God,
In a Yom Kippur wilderness
Of heartbreak and isolation,
Of fire and ash,
Of lurking plague,
Of fears unknown,
Of fears too real,
Where the shofar blast
Is a faint echo,
And the still small voice
Waits in stillness.

Here we stand
Renewing our vows,
To love and seek God,
To love and support our people,
To build a world of justice and peace.
We will never
Rescind or revoke,
Revise or renege,
Abandon or discard,
Our vows, oaths,
Pledges, duties, commitments
To You,
Not last year,
Not this year,
Not next year,
Never.

Return to us, Holy One,
As we return to You.
With or without an answer
To our questions and supplications,
We will sing tonight in the name
Of the God of mercy.

אוֹר זָרֻעַ לַצַּדִּיק וּלְיִשְׁרֵי־לֵב שִׂמְחָה.
Or zarua latzadik, ulyishrei lev simchah.
Light is sown for the righteous, and gladness
for the upright in heart.

All Mitzvot: A Kol Nidrei *Meditation*

All mitzvot, blessings, good deeds, repairs, regrets,
Offerings, kindnesses, courtesies, confessions,
Apologies, appeasements, admissions, amends,
Moments of grace, of joy, of sharing, of charity,
Moments of gratitude and moments of love,

מִיּוֹם כִּפּוּרִים שֶׁעָבַר עַד יוֹם כִּפּוּרִים זֶה

Miyom kipurim she-avar ad yom kipurim zeh
From last Yom Kippur until this Yom Kippur
I offer to You, Source of blessings,
In humble aspiration,
For they are now given to heaven
And are without merit to me on earth,

מִיּוֹם כִּפּוּרִים זֶה עַד יוֹם כִּפּוּרִים הַבָּא

Miyom kipurim zeh ad yom kipurim haba
From this Yom Kippur until the next,
So I might hear Your command
And remember my unavoidable vow
To use my gifts
As tools to heal the world.

וַיֹּאמֶר יהוה: סָלַחְתִּי כִּדְבָרֶךָ.

Vayomer Adonai: "Salachti, kidvarecha."
And Adonai said: "I have pardoned, as you have asked."

Prayer for My Congregation

God of Old,
Bless our holy congregation
During these days of awe,
These days of judgment,
These days of forgiveness.
We are Your servants,
The old and the young,
The poor and rich,
Lovers of Torah,
The strong and the infirm,
Teachers and students,
Lovers of Your way,
Beautiful in our imperfection,
Doing Your will when joy surrounds us,
Doing Your will, even yet, when our hearts are broken.

God whose name is Mercy,
God whose name is Truth,
Our lives are in Your hands.
Our time is fleeting.
You number our days.
Grant our congregation steadfast compassion,
Enduring devotion,
Strength, wisdom, and kindness.
Let us celebrate together with fullness of heart.
Let us mourn together under a tent of comfort and care.
Let us serve You from generation to generation,
So that our days are filled
With hope,
With love,
With Your Holy Word.

I Walked with God

For a fraction
Of a fraction
Of a moment,
I walked with You.
It began
And ended
So quickly
That it was gone
Before I felt
Your presence.
How is that fair?
How is that kind?
To answer my yearning
With desire.
To answer my longing
With emptiness.
To leave me with only
A shadow of a memory.
To wonder what
Could have been
Were I ready
For You.
Or maybe,
Just maybe,
You are asking
Me to remember,
To always remember,
How close
We can be.

Hints of God

Look for hints of God
In all that is,
In all that was,
In all that will be.
For God radiates
From your life
And from your face,
The holiness that infuses us all.
This is the legacy,
The gift forever given,
Passed on from mother to child,
From father to babe,
Visible in your countenance
And in your way of being.
Look for God
Inside yourself,
And you will see holiness
In everyone and everything.

The Path to God

The path to God
Is not invisible,
But it is not so clear, either,
Not simple to find.

The path to God
Begins in your heart
And your breath,
In the space where
One heartbeat begins
And another ends,
The place where
The outbreath yields to the inbreath
And the inbreath yields to the outbreath.

The path to God
Is the journey of your life.
The path to God
Is the way home.

Shofar Blasts/*Shofarot*

The Holy One of Blessing said: ". . . On
Rosh HaShanah recite before Me verses that
mention Sovereignty, Remembrances, and
Shofarot. Sovereignty so that you will crown
Me as Sovereign over you. Remembrances so
that your remembrance will rise before Me
for good. And with what will the remem-
brance rise? It will rise with the shofar."
—Babylonian Talmud, *Rosh HaShanah* 16a

Let Your Heart Stir

Glory in the sound of the shofar.
Let the trumpet of our people
Be the voice of your heart.
For your soul knows the call.
Let your heart stir
And your eyes open, anew.

Revel in the sweetness of the new year.
The delight of healing,
The joy of possibility,
The pleasure of being.
Let your heart stir
And your eyes open, anew.

Exalt in the triumph of forgiveness.
Let the glory of repentance
Be the light of your days,
For your spirit knows the way home.
Let your heart stir
And your eyes open, anew.

The Sound of Holiness

When God, in creating,
Began to create,
Silence hovered over the face of the deep.
And God said,
T'kiah. T'ruah. T'kiah.

Holiness has a sound.
Part swoosh of blood in the veins,
Part hum from the edge of the universe,
Part stillness, part vibration,
Part life entering a newborn,
Part life leaving the deceased,
Part dissonance, part resonance,
A sound that can only be heard
With the heart.

When God, in creating,
Began to create,
God spoke in music,
Giving us the shofar
As a vessel to hold the divine voice
And as an instrument
To summon awe and wonder,
So we might become,
In our own lives
And in the world,
T'kiah g'dolah.

The Path of Righteousness

God of what was and what will be,
Of what might have been and might still be.
God of past and future,
Of memories and beginnings.
God of the finite and the infinite,
Of moments and possibilities.
What is my life?
And what of my death?
What of my choices?
And what of my future?
What of this distance?
And what of the endless sky?
What of the darkness?
And what of the light?

God of the seen and unseen,
Of the known and unknowable.
Teach me patience and understanding
As the mysteries of my life unfold.
Teach me to live gently, love generously,
And to walk with strength and confidence.
Teach me to give and to receive,
Sharing Your blessings in joy and sorrow.
Teach me to see others through Your eyes,
As children of God.
And teach me to see myself and my life as You do,
With love.

Blessed are You, Adonai,
Source of life,
Guardian and Shelter,
You set Your people on the path of righteousness,
Holiness and charity,
Kindness and grace,
To return to You in service.
Blessed is Your holy name.

Clear a Road

קוֹל קוֹרֵא בַּמִּדְבָּר פַּנּוּ דֶּרֶךְ יהוה יַשְּׁרוּ בָּעֲרָבָה מְסִלָּה לֵאלֹהֵינוּ.

*Kol korei: "Bamidbar panu derech Adonai, yashru b'aravah
m'silah l'Eloheinu."*

A voice rings out: "Clear in the desert a road for Adonai.
Level in the wilderness a highway for our God!"

Clear a road
In your heart
For God.
Set in your soul
A highway
To holiness.
Then righteousness
Will enter your days
To cleanse your spirit
Of sorrow and distress,
And repentance
Will fill your thoughts,
Releasing your mind
Of anger and sin.

Lay the foundations
Of prayer and song,
Of peace and humility,
Of surrender and love,
So that your life
Becomes a path
To mystery and wonder.
Then forgiveness
Will open before you,
Stretching forth
From your hands
To the horizon.

Without a Sound

I whispered a secret prayer to God,
Who whispered a secret answer to me,
So quietly
That it arrived
In the chambers of my soul
Without a sound.

Oh how I wish to hear Your voice.
Oh how I wish to know Your dreams for me.
Oh how I wish to let my heart run wild and free,
As light as a bird song,
As true as the call of the shofar,
As certain as an angel calling out holy, holy, holy . . .

I whispered a secret prayer to God,
Who whispered a secret answer to me,
To trust
That blessings arrive
In the chambers of my soul
Without a sound.

An Hour of Compassion

Let this
Be an hour
Of compassion
From heaven,
And let it be
A time of favor
Throughout the earth.

Let this
Be an hour
Of compassion
For all who seek You,
And let it be
A time of favor
For all who yearn for You.

Let this
Be an hour
Of compassion
Among Your children.
Let it be
A time of favor,
A time for peace.

תְּהֵא הַשָּׁעָה הַזֹּאת שְׁעַת רַחֲמִים וְעֵת רָצוֹן מִלְפָנֶיךָ.
T'hei hashaah hazot sh'at rachamim v'eit ratzon mil'fanecha.
Let this hour be an hour of compassion and a time of
favor before You.

Sovereignty/*Malchuyot*

Rabbi Akiva descended before the ark
[during a drought] and said, "*Avinu Malkeinu*,
we have no Sovereign other than You. *Avinu
Malkeinu*, for Your sake, have mercy on us."
And rain immediately fell.

> —Babylonian Talmud, *Taanit* 25b

Rav said, "Any blessing that does not contain
mention of God's name is not a blessing."
And Rabbi Yochanan said, "Any blessing that
does not contain mention of God's sovereignty
is not a blessing."

> —Babylonian Talmud, *B'rachot* 40b

God's Plan: An Introspection

If God's plan
Followed my plan,
I would have no scars on my skin
Or in my heart.

If God's plan
Followed my plan,
I would not have felt the fire or the ice,
Heard the beauty or the terror,
Seen the new bud or the dying leaf.

If God's plan
Followed my plan,
I would not have learned to grieve or to cherish,
To hope or surrender,
To be broken and still be whole.

What, then, keeps me locked in fear,
In dread of yielding to Your great works,
Your awesome love,
Your radiant power?
What small desire,
Petty hope—
What yearning of self—
Blocks my service in God's holy name?

God on high,
Release me from my judgments and designs.
Open my heart to You fully,
Without reservation.
Cast out my doubts and shames,
So I may receive Your divine wisdom and strength.

God of all being,
Make my limbs Your tools and
My voice Your messenger.
Make my heart Your tabernacle,
A dwelling place of holiness
And splendor.

Distances

God of patience,
I have kept myself
Distant from You,
Locking up
Pieces of my heart,
Yet I have demanded Your presence
In my times of need.

Sometimes You seem so far away—
Unreachable, unfindable, unknowable—
That my love of You feels foolish.
Sometimes You are so close
That I can barely breathe,
Overwhelming my thoughts,
Flooding my senses.

Sovereign of the universe,
Too far to reach,
Too close to see,
Lead me back to You.

Eternity

Eternity
Whispers compassion
With a still small voice,
Wondering
If the music of awe
Will be heard.

Eternity
Thunders righteousness
With a blast of the shofar,
Wondering
If the music of holiness
Will be understood.

Eternity
Sings love
With the majesty of Torah,
Knowing
That the music of God
Plays on.

Foundation and Sky

God,
You are Foundation and Sky,
Rock and Storm,
Now and Forever,
Bedrock and Moonlight,
Ocean and Wind,
Creator and Sovereign,
Eternal and Eternity.

Let the river of Your blessings
Wash me clean,
So that I do Your will
With steady hands
And an upright heart.

God,
You are Source and Shelter,
My Strength and my Destination,
The Way and the Path,
The Noun and the Verb,
The Object and the Subject,
Justice and Mercy,
Eternal and Eternity.

Let the river of Your blessings
Wash me clean,
So that I bring holiness into the world
With humility and joy,
In Your holy name.

Let Prayers Rise

God of all,
Source of mysteries,
Paramount over worlds,
Creator of heaven and earth,
Let my praises rise to meet You,
In the hidden and in the revealed,
In the sacred and in the mundane,
In Your presence and in Your absence,
In my faith and in my questions,
So that my love
Might always find You,
So that my heart
Might always yearn for You.

Let my praises
Flow like living waters
From the well of sacred music
To the secret chambers
Of Your abundance and blessings.

To Be Remembered by God

Praying to the heavens
For blessings,
Praying for the divine will
To bring peace
To this world of war and terror,
We recall how God remembered
Our ancestors,
Time and again.

God,
You remembered
Noah after the Flood.
You remembered the Hebrew slaves
And the promise
Of their deliverance
That You made to our ancestors,
Our Matriarchs and our Patriarchs.
You remembered Rachel and Hannah,
Each yearning for a child.
You pledged to remember Ephraim—
The whole House of Israel—
With tenderness.

God who remembered
Our ancestors
Time and again
In the days old,
The pain of feeling
Forgotten by You
Rends my heart.

Remember us,
As we remember You,
On this day of awe and judgment.

וְנֶאֱמַר: טֶרֶף נָתַן לִירֵאָיו יִזְכֹּר לְעוֹלָם בְּרִיתוֹ.
V'ne-emar: "Teref natan lirei-av; yizkor l'olam b'rito."
As it is written: "God sustains the reverent;
God remembers the covenant forever."

וְנֶאֱמַר: וְזָכַרְתִּי אֲנִי אֶת בְּרִיתִי אוֹתָךְ
בִּימֵי נְעוּרָיִךְ וַהֲקִימוֹתִי לָךְ בְּרִית עוֹלָם.
V'ne-emar: "V'zacharti ani et b'riti otach bimei n'urayich,
vahakimoti lach b'rit olam."
As it is written: "I will remember the covenant I made with
you in the days of your youth, and I will establish it with
you as an everlasting covenant."

כָּאָמוּר: וְזָכַרְתִּי לָהֶם בְּרִית רִאשֹׁנִים אֲשֶׁר הוֹצֵאתִי אוֹתָם
מֵאֶרֶץ מִצְרַיִם לְעֵינֵי הַגּוֹיִם לִהְיוֹת לָהֶם לֵאלֹהִים אֲנִי יהוה.
Ka-amur: "V'zacharti lahem b'rit rishonim, asher hotzeiti otam
mei-eretz Mitzrayim—l'einei hagoyim—liyot lahem l'Elohim;
ani Adonai."
As it is said: "I will remember for their sake the covenant of
the ancients, whom I freed from the land of Egypt—in the
sight of the nations—to be their God; I, Adonai."

Crown

Let my life be a crown
Upon the Torah.
And let Torah
Be the crown of my life.
My heart will overflow
With God's teachings,
My hands will become
A fountain of God's blessings,
And my soul will give testimony
To the glory of God's holy word.

Sin and Regret

Rabbi Abahu said, "In the place where peni-
tents stand, even the completely righteous do
not stand."
                    —Babylonian Talmud, *B'rachot* 34b

Their status is even higher than that of those
who never sinned, for they subdue the evil
inclination more than the others.
                    —*Orchot Tzaddikim* 26

An Easy Sin

A sin so easy to practice,
Each moment, without awareness,
Is failure to see
The miracle of each new day
Or to fill our days with hope
And love.

The roots of sin
Are hatred and idle hands.

A sin so easy to practice,
Each moment, without awareness,
Is failure to see
The miracle of each new breath
Or to fill each breath with joy
And service.

The roots of holiness
Are love and work.

God of wisdom,
Grant me the ability
To see the flow of miracles around me,
In awe and wonder,
So that I become of vessel of Your glory
And an instrument of Your holy name.

Then I will rejoice,
Rededicating my life to You
With prayer
And with deeds of loving-kindness.

Fear

God of veiled mystery,
God of hidden destinations,
I've walked through jet-black nights
Waiting for the hint of dawn.
I've climbed the silent trail
Hoping to discover another wandering soul.
I've risen at daybreak
To conquer fierce winds and shifting snows.
I live between moments of power and moments of despair,
Between victory and defeat,
Between crushing losses and uncertain futures.

Fear is a memory.
Fear is a warning.
Fear offers a choice.

Holy One,
God who placed challenges and triumphs
In the path of the righteous
And at the feet of our ancestors,
Help me to see my fear as a tool,
As a source
And as a friend.
Let fear be my calling to bravery,
An invitation to vitality and strength.

Blessed are You, God of trials and victories,
Who created fear as the pathway to power.

Doubt

God of ancient secrets,
God of unknown futures,
I've been on the mountain
And in the valley.
I've swum calm waters
And been tossed by a raging sea.
I've held moments of perfect faith
And been consumed by impenetrable doubt.
I live between moments of clarity and hours of confusion,
Between daylight and twilight.
I live between the heights and the depths,
Between the calm and the storm,
Between hesitation and trust.

Doubt is a gift.
Doubt is a messenger.
Doubt is a doorway.

Holy One,
Creator of mysteries beyond my grasp,
Help me to see my doubts as teachers and guides
Leading me back to You,
Your people,
And Your Word.
Let my doubt be the gateway to faith,
Just as confusion is the path to understanding,
As night is the doorway to sunlight.

Blessed are You, Redeemer of the lost,
Who created doubt so that we might discover faith.

Anger

God of the inner journey,
Source of strength,
I've been assaulted by an unseen foe
And comforted by a steadfast friend,
Cut down in the name of love,
Lost in confusion and dismay,
Blinded by a wave of rage
And soothed by gentle breathing.
I live between moments of desperate anger
And days of boundless joy,
Between a heart of war
And a soul of peace.

Anger is a defense.
Anger is power.
Anger is intensity.

Holy One,
God whose gifts challenge my understanding,
Open my eyes to injustice
And let my anger become a source of energy
Channeled toward building and healing.
Let anger be a gateway to *tikkun olam*
So I become a force for holiness and love.

Blessed are You, Source of wisdom,
Who created anger to illuminate the path to justice.

Shame

God of my heart,
Source of my spirit,
I've been swallowed by a dirge
And elevated by songs of celebration.
I've judged myself harshly
And given myself grace.
I've climbed to see the glorious sunset
And have laid low, shivering against a pounding storm.

I live between moments of joyous surrender
And times of lonely isolation,
Between calm and storm,
Between shame and wonder.

Shame is a mirror.
Shame is a portal.
Shame is a guide.

Holy One,
God of mysteries beyond my understanding,
Help me to see my shames as teachers and guides,
As reminders of my sacred humanity,
Leading me to a vision of my best self.
Let shame be the gateway to truth
So that I may release it without fear,
In awe and righteousness.

Blessed are You, Redeemer of the lost,
Who created shame so that we might discover the path
to wisdom.

Allow Your Heart to Break

How courageous you must become
To allow your own heart
To break
Under the burden
Of your wrongs and misdeeds,
So that you might confess,
In earnest,
To yourself,
To others,
To God.

How courageous you must become
To allow your own heart
To heal
With the balm
Of amends and repair,
So that you might return,
In earnest,
To yourself,
To others,
To God.

How courageous you must become
To live your life
As a blessing,
To open your heart,
In the fullness of love
And dedication,
To yourself,
To others,
To God.

Sin Offering

I stand before You this day
God of Old,
To offer my sins
As tribute to my humanity,
To offer my repentance
As tribute to my holiness.
Teach me to cast off these sins,
To make space for Your radiance and light,
To make space for my humanity and this holiness
To meet in the core of my being,
So that my soul may shine brighter.
So that the works of my hands
Will praise Your creation.
So that my years will be a blessing
In heaven and on earth.
I stand before You this day,
God of Old,
To choose life.

Confession/*Vidui*

Rabbi Abahu said about this, "'We will pay
bulls with our lips' (Hosea 14:3). What will
we pay in lieu of bulls and in lieu of the scape-
goat? It is our lips."

—*Shir HaShirim Rabbah* 4:4

All of the commandments in the Torah,
whether they be the positive commandments
or the negative, if a person transgressed any
of them, whether intentionally or uninten-
tionally, when they repent and return from
sinning, they are obligated to confess before
God.

—Maimonides, *Mishneh Torah*,
Laws of Repentance 1:1

Meditation Before Vidui

God of Old,
Judge and Sovereign,
Healer and Guide:

Today I recount my deeds—
The sins I've committed,
The blessings I've bestowed.

Today I recall my year—
The challenges I've faced,
The decisions I've made.

Today I reach into my heart—
The moments of anger,
The moments of love.

By Your command,
God of mercy,
I lay bare the secrets within me,
Light and darkness,
My gentle hand and my clenched fist,
My strength and conceit,
Anger and fear.

By Your command,
God of wisdom,
I open myself to see truth,
Beauty and degradation,
The holy and the profane,
The victorious and the guilty.

By Your command,
God of salvation,
I reclaim all that I am
And all that I've done,
My pride and my shame,
Returning to You
So that I may redeem my days
With awe and righteousness.

Not Ready

I am not ready
To confess to myself
All that I have done
To add brokenness to Your world.
How, then, can I be ready
To confess to You?

The day has come.
The shofar will blast.
The still small voice will whisper in my ear.
I know this.
And I am still not ready
To confess to myself,
To confess to You.

But, oh,
How these lists of sins and transgressions
Call to memory my own failings,
Striking my heart to revive my soul.
Perhaps I am finally open enough
To examine my life.
To introspection.
To Your guidance.
Perhaps I am finally open enough
To declare that I will amend my ways
And take that resolution into the world
With fierce dedication
To Your holy calling.

Guilt That Isn't Mine

God of compassion,
Why is misunderstanding between people
So difficult to repair
When our intentions are good
And our desire is for amends?
Perhaps because boundaries,
Important and fragile,
Can be disregarded so easily.

I have been accused of insensitivity,
Unwillingness to be present as desired,
Inflexibility, selfishness.
But my boundaries were clear,
My intention shared,
And a demand was made anyway.
In these moments of contrasting interpretations
And misunderstandings,
Why do I accept guilt that isn't mine?
Why do I want to please and placate?
What part of myself am I willing to give away
To repel the accusation?

God of kindness,
I pray to change no one but myself,
Allowing others their interpretations
While allowing myself
Freedom from their judgments,
Respecting my own boundaries and needs,
In the fullness of self-respect and self-care,
With no malice toward the other,
But with gentleness of spirit,
Faith in friendship,
And a heart of peace.

Am I Ready?

Am I ready
To cast away my sins,
The little loves
That I cling to
That help me survive,
The ones that I hold on to
Year after year,
That I pretend
Do no harm,
To me,
To others,
To God?

Am I ready
To cast away my sins,
The accidental
And the purposeful
Misdeeds that I refuse
To amend,
So that I can stay
Comfortable
In the discomfort
Of my transgressions?

Am I ready,
Finally ready,
To be free?

Failures of Joy

These are the gifts
Of joy and service
Whose fruits are without measure,
Whose blessings are beyond counting,
Which we failed to enjoy:
For the sin we committed against You
   by neglecting our parents.
For the sin we committed against You
   by skimping on our Jewish learning.
For the sin we committed against You
   by closing our doors to guests.
For the sin we committed against You
   by disregard for the sick.
For the sin we committed against You
   by indifference to the marriage chuppah.
For the sin we committed against You
   by missing funerals and shivahs.
For the sin we committed against You
   by inattention to prayer.
For the sin we committed against You
   by creating strife with others.
For the sin we committed against You
   by neglecting Torah study, which—with a full heart—
Leads to them all.

Forgiveness Inside

This I confess to myself:
I have locked forgiveness away,
Hiding its wonder and grace
In a secret spot deep in my heart.
I have set myself up as judge and accuser,
As provocateur and jury,
Regarding my own words and deeds,
My wisdom and my truth,
With loathing and with disdain.
I have known forgiveness from God,
But not from myself.

God of redemption,
With Your loving and guiding hand
Seeking forgiveness is easy.
Accepting forgiveness is a struggle.
In Your wisdom You have given me this choice:
To live a life of condemnation,
Or to set my heart free to love You,
To love Your people,
And to love myself.

God of mercy, help me to leave my judgments behind,
To hear Your voice,
To accept Your guidance,
And to see the miracles in each new day.

Blessed are You,
God of righteousness,
In Your wisdom You have taught us
That forgiveness is the road to peace.

Repentance/*T'shuvah*

Rabbi Chama bar Chanina said, "Great is
repentance, as it brings healing to the world."
... Rabbi Levi said, "Great is repentance,
as it reaches the heavenly throne."... Rabbi
Yochanan said, "Great is repentance, as it
overrides even a prohibition of the Torah."
... Rabbi Yonatan said, "Great is repentance,
which hastens redemption."... Reish Lakish
said, "How great is repentance, for it turns
sins into merits."... Rabbi Yonatan said,
"Great is repentance, which lengthens the
years of a person's life."... Rabbi Meir said,
"How great is repentance! On the merit of
one person who repents, the entire world is
forgiven."

—Babylonian Talmud, *Yoma* 86a–b

Repentance Inside

This I confess:
I have taken my transgressions with me,
Carrying them year by year into my hours and days,
My lapses of conscience
And indiscretion with words,
My petty judgments
And my vanity,
Clinging to grief and fear, anger and shame,
Clinging to excuses and to old habits.
I've felt the light of heaven,
Signs and wonders in my own life,
And still will not surrender to holiness and light.

God of redemption,
With Your loving and guiding hand
Repentance in prayer is easy.
Repentance inside,
Leaving my faults and offenses behind,
Is a struggle.
In Your wisdom You have given me this choice:
To live today as I lived yesterday,
Or to set my life free to love You,
To love Your people,
And to love myself.

God of forgiveness, help me to leave my
   transgressions behind,
To hear Your voice,
To accept Your guidance,
And to see the miracles in each new day.

Blessed are You,
God of justice and mercy,
You set Your people on the road to *t'shuvah*.

Regarding Old Wounds

Daughter of man,
Son of woman,
Child of humanity:
Your wounds are deep,
Your losses crushing,
Knife on flesh,
Hammer on bone,
Burning your heart and searing your eyes.
Why do you invite them back
To chastise your days
And torture your nights?
Why do you love these old wounds,
Holding them so dear?

Son of celebration,
Daughter of ecstasy,
Child of compassion and sacred secrets:
Cast off your doubts,
Banish your fears,
Exile the pain of time beyond your reach.
There is beauty in your past,
Wonder in your future,
And holiness in each new moment of life.

Come, you children of God,
You witnesses to suffering and grace,
Lift your heads from your hands,
Raise your voices in song,
Lift your lives in service,
And rekindle the light of compassion and love.
Then your lives will become a blessing,
A well of hope,

A river of consolation,
A fountain of peace.

Blessed are You, God of forgiveness,
You renew our lives with purpose.

Who, Still Broken

Who by fire,
Screaming with seared flesh?
Who by water,
Gasping for one more breath?

Rock of life,
Tell me that these are not
Your tools of justice.
Tell me that these are not
Your verdicts or Your punishments.
How do You bear the cries
Of Your children?
The starving,
The battered,
Buried in rubble
Or washed to sea?

No, this is not my God.
Neither Judge nor Witness,
Prosecutor nor Executioner,
Issuing severe decrees
In a kangaroo court
Of intimidations
And forced confessions.

כִּי כְשִׁמְךָ כֵּן תְּהִלָּתֶךָ.
Ki k'shimcha kein t'hilatecha.
For according to Your name,
So is Your praise.
Your name is Righteousness. Forgiveness. Love.
Your names are Mother, Father, and Teacher.
Your names are Source and Shelter.

קָשֶׁה לִכְעוֹס וְנוֹחַ לִרְצוֹת.
Kasheh lichos v'no-ach lirtzot.
You are slow to anger
And ready to forgive.
But I,
I am slow to change,
Slow to amend my ways.
I can be consumed by the fire
Of my own anger.
I can drown in the sea
Of my own sorrow.
I need Your guidance,
Your gentle hand.

וְאַתָּה הוּא מֶלֶךְ, אֵל חַי וְקַיָּם.
V'atah hu Melech, El chai v'kayam!
For You are forever our living God and Sovereign!

Yes, I will fall to my knees
Before You.
For You are holy,
Your majesty fills the universe.
My origin is dust
And I will return to dust.
Until then,
God of mercy,
תְּשׁוּבָה, תְּפִילָה, וּצְדָקָה
T'shuvah, t'filah, utzdakah—
Repentance, prayer, and righteousness—

Will allow me to rise,
To stand before You.
Human,
Humble,
Fallible,
Still broken,
And still whole.

My Repentance

What is my repentance?
And what is my return?
My repentance is for moments wasted.
My return is to You.
My repentance is for forgotten love.
My return is to life.
My repentance is for abandoning mitzvot.
My return is to Torah.

What is my repentance?
And what is my return?
My repentance is for mistakes, oversights, and failures past.
My return is to prayer, righteousness, and *tikkun olam.*

Join Me

Come with me today,
God of Old,
Join me on this journey

Lead me in my thoughts.
Lead me in my words.
Lead me in my deeds.

Guide me to strength and purpose.
To vision and insight.
To gentleness and love.

Come with me today,
God of our mothers,
God of our fathers,
Show me the path
To wisdom and holiness.

Lead me in my heart.
Lead me in my breath.
Lead me in my being.

Restore me to Torah and mitzvot,
To righteousness and charity,
To justice and mercy,
A life of blessings,
Abundant in grace,
Overflowing with beauty,
Hands of healing,
Eyes of love,
A soul of peace,
In service to You,
Enthroned in my spirit.

God of Israel,
We return to You
With humility,
Our Rock, our Shield,
Our Comfort, our Guide,
Our journey home.

Cry No More

Cry no more for the sins of the past.
Rejoice in your repentance and your return.
For this is the day God made,
To lift you up from your sorrow and shame,
To deliver you to the gates of righteousness.

Remember this:
Love is the crown of your life
And wisdom the rock on which you stand.
Charity is your staff
And justice your shield.
Your deeds declare your kindness
And your works declare your devotion.

Cry no more for your fears and your dread.
Rejoice in your blessings and your healing.
For this is the day that God made,
To raise your countenance and hope,
To deliver you to the gates of holiness.

The Silence That Speaks

קוֹל דְּמָמָה דַּקָּה יִשָּׁמַע ...
A still small voice is heard ...
Kol d'mamah dakah yishama ...

Silence
Has a voice
Almost too thin
To be heard,
Except in
A willing heart.

Silence
Has a voice
Echoing
From the heavens,
Calling on you
To face yourself.

Silence
Has a voice
Resounding
From your heart,
Summoning you
To face God.

Silence has a voice,
Small and thin,
Calling out to you
To find holiness
And love,
Calling out to you
To seek what your God
Requires of you.

Small and Large

It's good
To be small
Inside,
So small
You might feel
The humility
Of your soul,
The surrender
Of your heart,
The wonder
Of your being.

It's good
To be large
Inside,
So large
You might feel
The grandeur
Of your soul,
The immensity
Of your heart,
The magnificence
Of your being.

It's good
To be small
Inside,
To repent and return

To your God.
It's good
To be large
Inside,
To pray for forgiveness
For all of Creation.

Forgiveness/*S'lichah*

Rabbi Elazar said, "Anyone who performs charity and justice is considered as though they have filled the whole world in its entirety with kindness."

—Babylonian Talmud, *Sukkah* 49b

Remembering My Humanity

I'm sorry, I said to God,
For all of the time I've wasted,
The bad choices I've made,
And for the moments I knew what to do
But did something else.

You're human, God said to me,
Exactly as I made you.

This is grace,
That God remembers
My humanity
Even when I forget,
Even when I hold myself to impossible standards,
Even when I want to punish myself
For my failings and faults.

You must learn to love yourself,
God said,
The way I love you,
With compassion and humor.
Then, when your heart
Yearns for forgiveness,
You will offer yourself,
And the world,
Kindness and grace.

To Be Free

Let the well of forgiveness
Wash me clean.
How I wish
To be free
Of evil thoughts and callous deeds.
How I wish
To be worthy in Your sight.
To receive a heart refreshed,
And a soul that shines.
To be free
Of iniquity, transgression, and sin.
To emerge from the waters of Your mercy,
Into the light of Your love.

When the Light Doesn't Shine

When you feel
That the light
Of God is not shining
On you
And you feel separated from life,
Perhaps you must find a way
To forgive yourself.

This bitterness
Is only a corruption of the truth,
That you are worthy
Of the breath of life.
That you are the obstacle
To your own glory.
That you are worthy
Of forgiveness.

There is no greater pain
Than to lose touch
With your own humanity
Or your divine spirit.
Let the light of God
Illuminate your days.
Let your eyes fill with holy fire.
Let your dream be
For redemption and return
To yourself and to your God.
Let your soul thirst for glory
And inspiration guide you.
For your soul yearns for life.
And your heart yearns to heal.

Forgiving God

It is not
In my power
To forgive God
For the pains and heartbreaks
Suffered in my life
Or the traumas
Suffered in the world.
For war and destruction.
For plague and terror.
For brutality and evil.

It is not
In my power
To pardon God,
For all that is callous or indifferent,
For all that is heartless or unkind,
For all that is baseless or random,
For all that is violent or cruel,
For all that appears unwanted, unbidden,
Without hope or blessing.

God's ways are hidden,
God's judgments are secret.
God's plan is veiled.

When I accept
That I cannot conceive
Of God's designs,
I surrender
Into the mystery
Of life.
Only then
Can I forgive
Myself.

Opposites and Antidotes

The opposite of doubt is love.
The antidote for fear is faith.

The opposite of uncertainty is surrender.
The antidote for hate is humility.

The opposite of restlessness is joy.
The antidote for grief is acceptance.

The opposite of certainty is wonder.
The antidote for confusion is awe.

The opposite of darkness is delight.
The antidote for boredom is beauty.

The opposite of judgment is curiosity.
The antidote for anger is forgiveness.

The High Priest

When the High Priest
Emerged from the Holy of Holies,
After reciting God's secret name,
Confessing for himself,
In fear and trembling,
Confessing for the priests,
Alone in God's sacred space,
Confessing for the community,
Seeking God's grace,
His countenance glowing
With the light of forgiveness,
His face shining with blessings,
The people of Israel
Rejoiced.

אֱמֶת מַה נֶּהְדָּר הָיָה כֹּהֵן גָּדוֹל בְּצֵאתוֹ
מִבֵּית קָדְשֵׁי הַקֳּדָשִׁים בְּשָׁלוֹם בְּלִי פֶגַע.

Emet mah nedar hayah Kohein Gadol b'tzeito
mibeit Kodshei HaKodashim b'shalom b'li fega.

Truly—how splendid a sight it was when the High Priest
came forth safe and in peace from the Holy of Holies!

Could it be
That one day
My heart will be so pure,
My soul so radiant,
After bringing supplication
And repentance
To the house of God,
With humility and surrender,
That my entire being

Will shine with joy and love?
Could it be
That one day
I will lift my life so high,
In loving service to the Divine,
That I breathe in beauty and wonder
And breathe out prayer and ecstasy?

Let wholeness and peace
Shine splendid
From our repentance and our return,
From the workings of our minds,
The longings of our hearts,
And the deeds of our hands,
So that our lives become
Beacons of hope
And lanterns of inspiration,
So that all will rejoice and sing:
"Truly, how splendid a sight,
The people of Israel,
After we call out to our God
To redeem our hearts
And renew our lives."

Why Forgive?

Forgiveness
Is a gift of love
To those who have wronged us,
Even when it seems
Impossible to find it inside ourselves
Or give to another.
High crimes of theft and violence.
Misdemeanors of pettiness and aggression.
High crimes of abuse and neglect.
Misdemeanors of provocation and indifference.
Sins of commission.
Sins of omission.

How they strike at the core
Of hope and love.
How they wear away
Our peace and serenity.

Why forgive
The unapologetic,
Willfully blind to the pain they inflict?
Why forgive
The apologetic,
Who continue still to cause suffering?

Forgiveness is a gift
That I give to myself
To release my life
From the harms of others
And the harms
I have perpetrated upon myself.

Forgiving the Unforgivable

Don't ask me
To forgive the unforgivable.
I am human,
The way You made me,
The dust of the earth
Animated by Your divine spirit
Subject to pain and loss beyond understanding,
Subject to violence and horrors beyond comprehension.

Don't ask me
To understand trauma or despair.
I am human,
Living in the world
As You made it,
Imperfect, incomplete,
Subject to the whips of humans,
Subject to the whims of history.

Yet You ask us
To suffer the consequences
Of Your creation,
The misdeeds and the horrors
Perpetrated brother against brother,
Sister against sister,
Human against human.

God of mercy,
Help me to remember
That You have given us the choice
To build or destroy,

To offer kindness or wretchedness,
To offer nobility or disdain,
To love freely or to hate without limit.

Perhaps then
I might be ready
To begin to forgive
You,
Myself,
Others.
Perhaps then
I might be ready
To breathe
Into wholeness again.

The Ancient Journey

One time I was walking along the path, and
I saw a young boy sitting at the crossroads.
And I said to him, "On which path shall we
walk to the city?" He said to me, "This path
is short and long, and that path is long and
short. I walked on the path that was short
and long." When I approached the city, I
found that gardens and orchards surrounded
it. I went back to the young boy again and
said, "My son, didn't you tell me that this way
is short?" He said to me, "And didn't I tell
you that it is also long?"

     —Babylonian Talmud, *Eiruvin* 53b

Village

Here once stood a village,
Rebuilt with stones
Of the village that stood before,
Which was built with the stones
Of the village before that,
Rebuilt and rebuilt,
Again and again,
Since memory began.
All that remains is an arched gate
Leading to the field and sky beyond.

Perhaps if you go through that gate
Your life will be torn down and rebuilt
By unseen forces calling you to enter.

This moment is a gateway
To mystery and wonder,
The place where past and future
Kiss the pulse of being,
Where everything and nothing meet
The vastness of now and forever.

Artifact

When you dig
In the landscape
Of your own heart,
You may find an artifact
Of your own past—
Something frightening
Or something beautiful—
That reveals
Your own ancient wisdom.

When you dig
In the landscape
Of the divine,
You may find an artifact
Of your own future—
Something glorious
Or something holy—
That shines like a gemstone
And blazes with hope,
Unexpected, powerful, unique,
The discovery that only you can find.

Winepress

If you pay attention
As you walk
Toward the gates
Of judgment and mercy,
You will see a winepress
As old as humanity.
This is the place
Where the messengers of God
Crushed your heart
And shattered your bones
To loose the glory within you,
The place where the finest libation
Of your spirit
Might be set free
To become an offering
To your God
And the world.

The pain,
Beyond imagining,
Still lingers,
But if you listen
As you walk,
You will hear the songs
Of the angels,
Glorious incantations
Of service to God,

The melodies that draw forth
From inside your heart,
Music that calls you
To wholeness and healing
After God's messengers
Draw the best of you
Into life.

These Ancient Stones

When these ancient stones whisper to us,
They yearn for our steadfast love.
They yearn for us to remember
How Israel walks through history
With justice and wisdom,
With righteousness and mercy.

God of our fathers and mothers,
Let compassion enter the land.

When these ancient stones whisper to us,
They yearn for our devotion and our service.
They yearn for us to remember the vision of our ancestors,
Their strength,
Their love of God and
Their love for our people.

God of generations,
Let tranquility enter the land.

When these ancient stones speak to us,
They pledge to stand firm
Against the tides of conquest, violence, and terror
That have assailed us
Throughout the millennia.
Yet they yearn for peace.
They yearn for us to learn
How to turn swords into plowshares
And spears into pruning hooks.

God of all being,
Let peace enter the land
And gladness enter our hearts.

Seeking God

God of my ancestors,
God of generations,
God beyond my understanding:
Who are You?
What are You?
Where are You?
Why do I struggle to reach You
When my quiet heart already knows You?
My calm thoughts
And open arms
Already know You.
My joy and pain,
Grief and love
Already know You.

Adonai my God,
Open me up to You
In celebration and surrender.
Reunite me with what I already know:
Your holiness and Your love.
Let Your word flow through me
So that I see and hear,
Taste, touch, and smell,
The beauty and blessings around me.
Then, God of Old,
I will remember to seek You always,
To praise You throughout the days,
And to honor You across the years.

Blessed are You, Holy One,
Hidden in plain sight,
Present in simple moments,
Present for eternity.

Ancient Dawn

Today you are
The ancient renewed,
The dawn of forever,
The rebirth of yourself,
The memory of who you are,
The wisdom of who you will become,
The holy revival of all that is good
And true
And wise.

Today you are
The call of forever,
The summons of tomorrow,
The rebirth of possibilities,
The journey to holiness,
The path of destiny,
The holy footsteps
That lead you home.

Do not flinch
From the brave and terrible
Journey to find yourself.
When you burn away
The dross that binds your heart,
You will emerge
Fresh and new
As you were
When God selected
A soul for you
From the gardens
Of glory.

History

History is sacred,
Memory is holy,
Time is a blessing,
Truth is a lantern.

Source of sacred moments,
Creator of time and space,
Teacher, Healer, and Guide:
Thank You for the gift of memory,
The gift that allows us to see beyond the present,
The gift that allows us to remember our past
And to remember our lives.

Thank You for the gift of vision,
The gift that allows us to imagine the future,
The gift that allows us to learn and to teach
The lessons of the ages,
The lessons of millennia,
So that we may heal ourselves and the world.

Eternal God,
Thank You for the gift of history,
The gift of ancient moments and modern tales.
Grant us the wisdom and understanding
To see history in the light of truth,
To trust the enduring power of memory
To guide us from generation to generation.

Frailty

God granted all the requests made by Moses
except one: to know why the righteous suffer.

—Babylonian Talmud, *B'rachot* 7a
(paraphrased in *The Koren Rosh
HaShana Mahzor*, 580)

Walking Toward Sunset

The sunrise is behind me now
As I walk toward sunset,
Curious to see
What is beyond
The horizon.

Ancient One,
Our lives move from birth to death,
From this world to the world-to-come.
Let this journey be for holiness and love,
For joy and laughter,
For hope and strength,
For service to Your holy name.

I am not ready, Holy One,
To lean over the edge
Of earth and sky
To see what You
Will do with me next,
And I know that the moment
Will be of Your choosing.

The sunrise is behind me now
As I walk toward sunset
I know that
God gives
And God takes away.
Blessed is God's holy name.

Look for Me

Look for Me where the sea meets the shore,
Where the sky finds the horizon,
Where the trees brush the sky.
Look for Me wherever heaven touches the earth.

Look for Me where lava pours from the core of a mountain,
Where water falls from the cliffs to the river,
Where flowers burst through cracks in the rocks.
Look for Me wherever heaven touches the earth.

Look for Me in the rhythm of your heart,
In the sigh of your breathing,
In the quiet of your soul.
Look for Me inside yourself,
In the drumming of your pulse,
The places where heaven touches you.

Unfinished Business

There is so much unfinished business in my life,
So much I have left undone.
Have I shown you my heart,
The well of love and sorrow,
Of fear and joy,
That I keep deep within?
Have I given you my hands,
The source of power and support,
Of gentleness and compassion,
As a gift of devotion?
Have I held you with my eyes,
The river of blessings
That flow as grace
From my core to yours?

There is so much unfinished business in my life,
To attend with joy and dancing,
Sending love from my soul to yours,
Now and forever.

To Relieve Fear

Frightened and alone,
I reach out to You, God of Ages,
To relieve the fear that crushes my hope
And drowns my laughter.
Grant me the fortitude
To accept Your solace and shelter,
To feel Your joy and love.
Release me from the bonds of my apprehensions
So that I might live with dignity and purpose.

God of Old,
You have made me in Your image
For a life of wonder and awe.
Renew my spirit.
Renew my heart.
Renew my faith.
Set me free.

God Arrives

And so,
God arrives,
And I am not ready.
God arrives,
And I am not listening.
Does the still small voice,
That quiet thin whisper,
That breath of silence,
Still pull me toward
Repentance, prayer, and charity?

And so,
Fear arrives,
And I am not ready.
Pain arrives,
And I am not ready.
What is this being human
That strikes at my safety,
At my security?
Who am I to yearn
For ease and comfort
When the world suffers?

And so,
Love arrives,
And I am finally ready.
Peace comes,
And I finally surrender.
God arrives,
And maybe, just maybe,
I will be ready to hear
The call to holiness

Before I return to dust.
Maybe, just maybe,
I will live open-hearted
Before I dry up like
A withered leaf,
Before I pass on
Like a cloud in the wind.

On the Day of My Death

What will I pray for
On the day of my death?
For you, dear ones, for you . . .

May your heart sing
And your eyes smile.
May your griefs vanish
And your joys soar.
Let blessings light your way,
And beauty guide your journey.
Let hope carry your days,
And wisdom lift your life.

As for me,
My journey has ended.
To those I've harmed, I'm sorry.
To you who've loved me, thank you.
To all I've met, bless you.
To the Source of being,
Let me return to You in peace.

My Rock

I have lost my grip
On You,
My Rock,
And I am lost at sea.
Perhaps, with a mighty hand
And an outstretched arm,
You will pull me back to safety.
Perhaps, with the great love
You have for Your people Israel,
You will bring me back to solid ground,
Where the feet of the righteous
Never stumble,
Where the mouths of the faithful
Are full of song.

Justice

Rabban Shimon ben Gamaliel used to say:
The world endures on three things—justice,
truth, and peace.

—Pirkei Avot 1:18

Hillel used to say: If I am not for myself, who
will be for me? And if I am for myself, what
am I? And if not now, when?

—Pirkei Avot 1:14

Is This the Fast?

Peace, peace,
To those who are upright,
Those who are steady,
Those who bring holiness
And light into the world.

Is this the fast that God desires?
To remember the homeless and the needy?
To bring healing into the streets
And justice into our courtyards?

Is this the sukkah we build?
To summon the hungry and forlorn?
To put food in the mouths of the poor
And bring strangers into our tents?

Is this the seder we host?
To end bondage in farm and factory?
To rally before the seats of power
In the name of the oppressed?

Is this the kashrut we keep?
To end mistreatment of flock and herd?
To live in harmony with the land
And use our resources wisely?

Is this the Torah we learn?
To hear the word of God
With humility and delight,
To thirst for truth and yearn for wisdom?

Is this the Shabbat we observe?
To shake off the bonds of the mundane?
To restore our lives
And renew our dreams of the world-to-come?

Is this the prayer we pray?
To cry out to the Holy One in joy and sorrow,
In the name of wholeness and healing,
In the name of peace?

Peace, peace,
In your gardens and in your groves,
In your houses and your villages,
For you will be called a delight,
A lamp of awe,
A beacon of wonder,
A source of healing,
And a well of inspiration,
Among your people Israel.

Why Do You Slumber?

מַה־לְּךָ נִרְדָּם?
Mah l'cha nirdam?
Why do you slumber,
Child of humanity?
When people die?
While children cry?
While anger shakes us?
When terror breaks us?
קוּם קְרָא אֶל־אֱלֹהֶיךָ!
Kum k'ra el Elohecha!
Get up, cry out to your God,
Cry out for justice and for peace.

מַה־לְּךָ נִרְדָּם?
Mah l'cha nirdam?
Why do you slumber,
Child of God?
Your heart is noble,
The need is global.
You have the power
In this desperate hour.
קוּם קְרָא אֶל־אֱלֹהֶיךָ!
Kum k'ra el Elohecha!
Get up, cry out to your God,
Cry out for justice and for peace.

מַה־לְּךָ נִרְדָּם?
Mah l'cha nirdam?
Why do you slumber,
Child of love?
The call is urgent,

The cry resurgent,
To embrace each other
And bless one another.
To rise from slumber.
To live in wonder.
קוּם קְרָא אֶל־אֱלֹהֶיךָ!
Kum k'ra el Elohecha!
Get up, cry out to your God,
Cry out for justice and for peace.

What to Cherish

Cherish not your triumphs
Nor your successes,
Nor the accolades that follow.
They are not seen nor heard on high.

Cherish the healing you bring to others,
The blessings you bestow,
Seen and unseen,
Heard and unheard,
The medicine your life brings to the world,
This resounds in heaven
And shakes the foundations of earth.
Mountains will dance,
Seas will rejoice,
And the sky will smile
When the joy of service
Is the source of your satisfaction
And the mission of your life.

Humble Before God

Humility
Before God
Is an act of spiritual bravery,
For you must
Surrender
To the wisdom and the will
Of the Unknown and Unknowable,
The Unseen and the Unseeable,
The Unfathomed and the Unfathomable.

Bend your knee
And lift your heart,
Bow your waist
And lift your spirit,
Prostrate your life
And exalt your being
In holiness and service
To the One
Who made heaven and earth.
Bring all that you are,
And place yourself
In God's holy presence,
On the altar of confession,
In the sanctuary of prayer,
In the temple of return,
To purify your heart
And renew your soul
In love and humble service
To your Maker,
Your people,
And the world.

Strive

Strive,
Torah says,
To be a beacon,
To be a light,
To stand up for justice.
Justice is the root of peace.

The day is short,
But it is yours.
The task is great,
But it is ours.
We will not be lazy in the work of righteousness.
And God is watching.

Strive in the name of healing,
Strive in the name of our children,
Strive in the name of heaven,
Strive in the name of earth.
Use your hands,
Use your voice,
Use your humanity,
To build a bridge from here
To a better world.

Where Is Mercy?

Adonai, Adonai—
God compassionate, gracious, and kind,
Showing mercy to the thousandth generation,
Where will we find Your mercy
In a world of war and plague,
Of pain and pandemic,
Of random killing and premeditated violence?
Where will we find
Your mercy,
When Your countenance
Stays hidden?

Mercy is now
In our hands,
In our deepest prayers,
And we will do
Your work of grace and kindness,
Providing healing
To a struggling world.
We are Your well of mercy,
And Your fountain of compassion.

Memory/*Yizkor*

Rabbi Yochanan said, "No righteous person
departs from this world until another compa-
rable righteous person is created."
    —Babylonian Talmud, *Yoma* 38b

On Lighting a Memorial Candle

A candle.
A flame.
A memory.

God of generations,
Grant a perfect rest under Your tabernacle of peace
To _____ [*name*],
Who has left this life and this world.
Let his/her/their soul find comfort.
Let his/her/their memory be a blessing.

This candle is for healing,
This flame is for hope,
Calling forth our joys and sorrows,
Calling forth our hours and our days.

God of our ancestors,
Bring me and my family solace and consolation
In this moment of remembrance.
Let all who mourn find peace.

For the Bereaved

Rock of Jacob,
Comfort of Rachel,
Broken and torn,
Shattered and crushed,
Bereaved and bereft,
We declare Your holy name.

We praise Your gifts and Your works.
You are Author and Artist,
Architect and Builder,
Source and Redeemer.

We, the mourners of Zion and Israel,
Comfort each other.
We console the lonely and embrace the lost.
We cry each other's tears.
Together we recall Your wonder and Your majesty.

Holy One,
Ineffable Redeemer,
Guiding Hand,
Gentle Hand,
Loving Hand,
Light of Israel,
You are our Shelter.

Mourner's Lament

In the morning whisper, heal me.
In the afternoon shout, help me.
In the evening ask, how long?

In the morning whisper, O love.
In the afternoon shout, O death.
In the evening ask, how long?

In the morning whisper, this again.
In the afternoon shout, no more.
In the evening ask, how long?

In the morning whisper, O love.
In the afternoon shout, O life.
In the evening ask, how long?

For Bereaved Children

Father of Jacob,
Mother of Rachel,
Source of awe and wonder,
Cradle and Shelter,
Our children are lost in tears,
Crushed in sorrow,
Erased in loneliness,
Bent and broken,
Their hopes, dust . . .
Their joys, cinders . . .
Their dreams, shadows.

You who comfort Zion and Israel,
Comfort our children in this moment of grievous loss,
And show them the path from darkness to light.
Renew their hope,
Rekindle their joy,
Spark their dreams,
So that they, too, will know Your healing power,
Your salvation and grace,
Your loving-kindness.
Hold them,
Lift them,
Carry them,
Until, refreshed by Your spirit,
They walk upright once again,
Toward holiness and love,
With charity and thanksgiving,
Humility and strength,
In awe and righteousness,
To sing Your praise.

Shoah Memorial Prayer

Creator of all,
Source and Shelter,
Grant a perfect rest under Your tabernacle of peace
To those who perished in the Holocaust,
Our fathers and mothers,
Our sisters and brothers,
Our rabbis and teachers,
Our neighbors and children,
The named and the unnamed,
Whose lives were cut off by
Brutal, vicious, cunning, calculated violence.
May they find peace in the world-to-come.
Remember the survivors who have since passed away
And the virtues of our people who have died at the hand
   of malice
In every generation.
We remember the works of their hands
And the messages of their hearts.
Bless the defenders of Israel with safety and strength
And the righteous of all nations who provide
Protection, shelter, and comfort to the Jewish people.
Let their deeds be a source of favor in heaven
And healing on earth.
Put an end to anger, hatred, and fear
And lead us to a time when no one will suffer at the hand
   of another,
Speedily, in our days.
May the memories of all who faced these horrors
Be sanctified with joy and love.
May their souls be bound up in the bond of life,
A living blessing in our midst.

O Auschwitz, O Birkenau

Treblinka, you will not see my tears.
Majdanek, you will not hear my sobs.
You will not wound me again.
You have done your evil.
You have taken your pounds of flesh.

Yes, I will shed tears for the lost,
The brutalized, the lynched,
The murdered, and the slain.
Not here,
Not inside your grounds,
Not inside your gates.
I'd rather choke on my sorrow
Than give it to you.

But Auschwitz, Birkenau,
You test my resolve.
You challenge my heart
Steeled against your evil,
Steeled against the echoes of mourning
That rise from your sullen earth.

When I leave the killing fields,
I will shout to the heavens.
I will lament with my people.
Our voices resounding with grief and power,
Unmistakable strength declaring,
"Come, you tyrants.
Come, you villains and antisemites,
You murderers and despots.
You have made us fearless, invincible.
We will survive you too."

Eileh Ezk'rah *After October 7*

אֵלֶּה אֶזְכְּרָה . . .
Eileh ezk'rah . . .
These I remember . . .

The young and the old,
The children, the mothers,
The babies, the fathers,
And I do not look away.
The brutalized, the maimed,
The assaulted, the raped,
Burnt alive,
Terrorized and tortured,
Killed and kidnapped,
And I do not look away.

עַל־אֵלֶּה אֲנִי בוֹכִיָּה . . .
Al-eileh ani vochiyah . . .
For these I weep . . .

In every age,
In our homes and our villages,
In the fields and on the streets,
In our cities and our towns,
Death and terror stalk . . .

עֵינִי עֵינִי יֹרְדָה מַּיִם . . .
Eini, eini yordah mayim . . .
My eyes, my eyes flow like streams of water . . .

For Re'im and Be'eri,
For Pittsburgh and Toulouse,
For Kfar Aza, Netiv HaAsara, and Nachal Oz,
For Mumbai and Colleyville,
For Ofakim, Nir Oz, Nirim, and Sderot,

For Paris and Poway,
For Alumim, Zikim, Psyduck, and Kissufim,
For Halle and Overland Park,
For Nir Yitzhak, Holit, and Sufa,
For every community,
In every generation . . .

אֵלֶּה אֶזְכְּרָה . . .
Eileh ezk'rah . . .
These I remember . . .

But how can I remember
What was stolen?
The loves, lost.
The dreams, lost.
Scientists, poets,
Artists, visionaries,
Leaders, learners,
Teachers of Torah,
The generations, lost.
The children of children,
And their children,
And theirs,
Never to be.

אֵלֶּה אֶזְכְּרָה וְנַפְשִׁי עָלַי אֶשְׁפְּכָה . . .
Eileh ezk'rah, v'nafshi alai eshp'chah . . .
These I remember,
I pour out my soul from within me . . .

And I call out . . .
יְיָ יְיָ אֵל רַחוּם וְחַנּוּן . . .
Adonai, Adonai, El rachum v'chanun . . .
God, God, compassionate and gracious . . .

Remember us.

At the Gates/N'ilah

God pays heed to tears, for the gates of tears
are never closed.

—*Kitzur Shulchan Aruch* 63:1

Rabbi Sh'muel said, "The gates of prayer are
sometimes open and sometimes closed, but
the gates of tears are never closed."

—*Midrash T'hillim* 4:3

Even though all the other gates of prayer may
be closed, the gates of tears are never closed.

—Babylonian Talmud, *Bava M'tzia* 59a

Rabbi Chanina said, "Everything is in the
hand of Heaven, except for fear of Heaven."

—Babylonian Talmud, *Nidah* 16b

The Entry to Our Hearts

Who mourns at the gates of righteousness
And dances at the gates of despair?
Who laughs at the gates of judgment
And cries at the gates of peace?
Who sings at the gates of misfortune
And howls at the gates of blessing?
Who shouts at the gates of mercy
And stands mute at the gates of penance?

Ancient One,
Source and Shelter,
We stand at the gates,
At the entry to our hearts,
At the passage to mystery,
At the crossroad of uncertainty.
Let these prayers be for healing.
Let these prayers be for life.

Blessed are You,
God of mercy,
You lead us from darkness to light,
From mourning to rejoicing,
From repentance to service,
So we may build our lives, anew.

Keep the Gates Open

Keep the gates open,
Holy One,
Keep them open a little longer,
So that my repentance and my yearning
May yet enter Your holy realm.

Keep the gates open,
Compassionate One,
So that our hearts may dwell,
To be refreshed in Your sacred space,
To be restored with justice and mercy,
To be nurtured and renewed with awe and wonder.

Rock of Israel,
Source and Shelter,
Keep the gates open,
So that when we leave this holy place
We remember
That wisdom and understanding surround us,
That peace and joy will yet follow,
That holiness and love will prevail.

Unlock the Gates

How does it feel
To yearn for God?
To yearn for sheltering wings?
To yearn to enter the palace of the Divine?
With all of your heart,
With all of your soul,
With all of your might?

How does it feel
To yearn for another?
To yearn for sheltering arms?
To yearn to enter the palace of love?
With all of your heart,
With all of your soul,
With all of your might?

How does it feel
To yearn for yourself?
To yearn for sheltering calm?
To yearn to enter the palace of peace?
With all of your heart,
With all of your soul,
With all of your might?

Ancient One,
I am outside the gates
Pounding on the door
As rain gathers
And night falls,

Where questions lurk
And fear trembles,
And my heart can no longer
Feel itself beating.

God, my God,
Will You help me crack the lock
That I, myself,
Have fastened
To the gates of mercy?

At the Gates

At the gates of repentance
You will be asked:
Are you ready to enter?
Are you ready to live a life of *t'shuvah*?

The gates of repentance
Surround my heart.
Unlock my fear,
God of Old,
So I may enter
The well of love
With wonder and awe.

At the gates of righteousness
You will be asked:
Are you ready to enter?
Are you ready to live a life of *tzedakah*?

The gates of righteousness
Surround my deeds.
Unlock my fortitude,
Source and Shelter,
So I may enter
The well of healing
With righteousness and strength.

At the gates of devotion
You will be asked:
Are you ready to enter?
Are you ready to live a life of *t'filah*?

The gates of devotion
Surround my spirit.
Unlock my faith,
Rock of Israel,
So I may enter
The well of mystery
With prayer and rejoicing.

Meditation Before N'ilah

Wait.
There is something else,
God of Old,
I must show You.
It's dark
And secret.
Part sadness.
Part anger.
Part fear.

Listen.
There is something else,
God of Old,
I must tell You.
It's hard
And heavy.
Part pride.
Part guilt.
Part shame.

Stay.
There is something else,
God of Old,
I need from You.
It's ancient
And new.
Part Torah.
Part mitzvot.
Part joy and love and light.

God of justice,
God of mercy,
Hear my plea.
Wait for me to return to You.
Listen as I confess to You.
Stay as I struggle to live my life as a blessing,
According to Your wisdom,
According to Your law,
According to Your word.

Your Gate

There is a gate
That is yours alone,
A gate that
Only you can open,
A gate of mystery,
A gate of longing,
The gate to your own heart.

Only you can open your heart to forgiveness,
Only you can open your life to love,
Only you can summon the holiness within.

There is a gate that God has
Given to you alone.
Open the gate.
Open the gate.
Let all that is good
And pure
And true
Flow through you.
Let all that is good
And pure
And true
Light your way home.

Permissions

The following are reprinted with permission from *These Words: Poetic Midrash on the Language of Torah* (CCAR Press, 2023): "The Sound of Holiness," "To Be Free," and "Where Is Mercy?" The following is reprinted with permission from *This Precious Life: Encountering the Divine with Poetry and Prayer* (CCAR Press 2021): "Is This the Fast?" The following are reprinted with permission from *This Joyous Soul: A New Voice for Ancient Yearnings* (CCAR Press 2019): "Without a Sound," "Sin Offering," and "For the Bereaved." The following are reprinted with permission from *This Grateful Heart: Psalms and Prayers for a New Day* (CCAR Press, 2017): "Sweet Cake," "The Path of Righteousness," "God's Plan: An Introspection," "Forgiveness Inside," "Repentance Inside," "Who, Still Broken," and "Cry No More."

The following are reprinted with permission from *Jewish Prayers of Hope and Healing* (Kavanot Press, 2013): "Seeking God," "For Bereaved Children," and "Shoah Memorial Prayer." "History" is reprinted with permission from *Haggadah Companion: Meditations and Readings* (Kavanot Press, 2014).

"Creation Sings" is used with permission of Cantor Erin Miles Frankel and AJ Luca.

Index of Liturgical Uses

This index provides the author's suggestions for matching works in this volume with the formal High Holy Day liturgy. Many of the prayer poems in this book fit with several rubrics of the liturgy and appear in multiple places in this index. Use this index along with the table of contents, which offers a theme-oriented arrangement of this work. This index is alphabetical, with the poetry in the volume itself arranged to flow from one prayer poem to the next. This index is based on the High Holy Day liturgy as found in *Mishkan HaNefesh: Machzor for the Days of Awe*.

Avinu Malkeinu/Almighty and Merciful
    The Archives of Heaven   28
    Hunger for God   35

Cheshbon HaNefesh/Accounting of the Soul
    Anger   80
    Artifact   128
    Doubt   79
    Fear   78
    God's Plan   65
    In Plain Sight   18
    Regarding Old Wounds   99
    Shame   81
    Unfinished Business   138
    Winepress   129

Eileh Ezk'rah/These I Remember
    Eileh Ezk'rah After October 7   163
    O Auschwitz, O Birkenau   162
    Shoah Memorial Prayer   161

For Victims of Terror
    Eileh Ezk'rah After October 7   163
    For Bereaved Children   160
    Forgiving God   116
    These Ancient Stones   131

Hin'ni/Here I Am
    Foundation and Sky   68
    Humble Before God   151
    My Rock   144
    Seeking God   132
    What to Cherish   151

Kol Nidrei/Release from Vows
    All Mitzvot: A *Kol Nidrei* Meditation   47
    Cry No More   106
    The Entry to Our Hearts   166
    These Vows   45
    Who Knocks?   39

N'ilah/Closing of the Gates
    The Book of Forgiving   26
    The Book of Living   27
    I Walked with God   49
    Keep the Gates Open   167
    Meditation Before *N'ilah*   172

Rosh HaShanah Evening/New Year
    Creation Sings   13
    Enter these Days   42

Meditation on the Eve of a New Year   5
Pervasive Peace   2
Sweet Cake   6
Wildly Unimaginable Blessings   3

Rosh HaShanah Day/New Year
Enter These Days   42
Hidden and Blessed   20
Hunger for God   34
In This Turning: A New Year's Day Meditation   9
A Moment of Blessing   15
A New Year Begins   7
Time Is the Gift   16

Seder HaAvodah/Discovering the Holy
Cry No More   107
The High Priest   119
Kneel and Rise   19
Of Psalm 27   33
Village   127

Sh'losh Esreih Midot/God's Thirteen Attributes
Draw Me Close   36
Hunger for God   35
On the Journey to You   37
Where Is Mercy?   154

S'lichot/Forgiveness
Forgiving God   116
Forgiving the Unforgivable   122
Opposites and Antidotes   118
Remembering My Humanity   113
To Be Free   114
When the Light Doesn't Shine   115
Why Forgive?   120

Tashlich

Allow Your Heart to Break 82

In Plain Sight 18

I Walked with God 49

Kneel and Rise 19

Of Psalm 27 33

Sin Offering 83

What to Cherish 151

T'filah Zakah/A Prayer for Purity and Worthiness

Am I Ready? 91

Distances 67

Draw Me Close 36

Foundation and Sky 69

Look for Me 138

My Repentance 103

Repentance Inside 98

Small and Large 108

Your Gate 174

T'filat HaLev/Prayer of the Heart

God's Plan 65

Hints of God 50

Join Me 104

Let Prayers Rise 70

On the Day of My Death 143

The Path to God 50

To Relieve Fear 140

Unlock the Gates 168

Walking Toward Sunset 137

When I Pray 41

T'kiat Shofar/Sounding of the Shofar

Clear a Road 59

An Hour of Compassion   61
Let Your Heart Stir   55
The Path of Righteousness   57
The Sound of Holiness   55
Without a Sound   60

Torah Service (Any)
  Crown   73
  Eternity   68
  Prayer for My Congregation   48

Torah Service, Rosh HaShanah
  Creation Sings   13
  Forgiving the Unforgivable   122
  To Relieve Fear   140

Torah Service, Yom Kippur Morning
  Is This the Fast?   147
  Sin Offering   83
  Strive   153

Torah Service, Yom Kippur Afternoon
  Ancient Dawn   133
  I Walked with God   49
  Why Do You Slumber?   149

Un'taneh Tokef/The Power of This Day
  At the Gates   170
  The Book of the Between   25
  The Book of the Righteous   24
  The Book of the Wicked   23
  Eternity   68
  God Arrives   141
  The Silence That Speaks   108
  Who, Still Broken   100

Vidui/Confession

Allow Your Heart to Break 82
Am I Ready? 91
An Easy Sin 77
Failures of Joy 92
Forgiveness Inside 93
Guilt That Isn't Mine 90
Meditation Before *Vidui* 87
Not Ready 89
Sin Offering 83

Yizkor/Memorial

Eileh Ezk'rah After October 7 163
For the Bereaved 158
For Bereaved Children 160
Mourner's Lament 159
On Lighting a Memorial Candle 157
O Auschwitz, O Birkenau 162
Shoah Memorial Prayer 161

Zichronot/Remembrance

History 134
To Be Remembered by God 71

Index of Hebrew References

This alphabetical index provides the sources for the Hebrew referenced in the prayer poems.

All Mitzvot: *Kol Nidrei* (*Mishkan HaNefesh: Machzor for the Days of Awe; Yom Kippur*, 18–20)

The Archives of Heaven: *Avinu Malkeinu* and *Sim Shalom* (*Mishkan HaNefesh: Machzor for the Days of Awe; Yom Kippur*, 252–53, 246)

Clear a Road: Isaiah 40:3

Eileh Ezk'rah After October 7: Psalm 42:5, Lamentations 1:16, Exodus 34:6 (*Mishkan HaNefesh: Machzor for the Days of Awe; Yom Kippur*, 516–17, 644)

The High Priest: *Avodah* service (*Mishkan HaNefesh: Machzor for the Days of Awe; Yom Kippur*, 508)

An Hour of Compassion: *Avinu Malkeinu* (*Mishkan HaNefesh: Machzor for the Days of Awe; Yom Kippur*, 428)

Of Psalm 27: Psalm 27:4 (*Mishkan HaNefesh: Machzor for the Days of Awe; Yom Kippur*, 124)

The Silence That Speaks: *Un'taneh Tokef* (*Mishkan HaNefesh: Machzor for the Days of Awe; Rosh HaShanah*, 174–82)

These Vows: Psalm 97:11 (*Mishkan HaNefesh: Machzor for the Days of Awe; Yom Kippur*, 16)

To Be Remembered by God: Psalm 111:5, Ezekiel 16:60, Leviticus 26:45 (*Mishkan HaNefesh: Machzor for the Days of Awe; Rosh HaShanah*, 265)

Where Is Mercy?: Exodus 34:5–7, God's Thirteen Attributes (*Mishkan HaNefesh: Machzor for the Days of Awe; Rosh HaShanah*, 228)

Who, Still Broken: *Un'taneh Tokef* (*Mishkan HaNefesh: Machzor for the Days of Awe; Rosh HaShanah*, 174–82)

Why Do You Slumber?: Jonah 1:6 (*Mishkan HaNefesh: Machzor for the Days of Awe; Yom Kippur*, 344)

About the Author

ALDEN SOLOVY is a modern-day *pay'tan*, a traveling poet/preacher/teacher who uses Torah and verse to engage and inspire. Alden embodies the intersection of scholarship and heart. His writings resonate with soul, and his presence is sought after in Jewish spiritual spaces around the world. A liturgist, lyricist, and educator, his work appears in both song and verse. Alden's work challenges the boundaries between poetry, song, meditation, personal growth, storytelling, and prayer. His writing was transformed by multiple tragedies, marked in 2009 by the sudden death of his wife. Alden's teaching spans from Hebrew Union College–Jewish Institute of Religion and the Conservative Yeshiva in Jerusalem to Limmud and Leo Baeck College in the United Kingdom, as well as synagogues throughout North America. He is the author of four volumes from CCAR Press: *These Words: Poetic Midrash on the Language of Torah* (2023), *This Grateful Heart: Psalms and Prayers for a New Day* (2017), *This Joyous Soul: A New Voice for Ancient Yearnings* (2019), and *This Precious Life: Encountering the Divine with Poetry and Prayer* (2021). *These Words* won a Silver Medal from the Independent Publisher Book Awards in the category of spiritual/inspirational. His work has also appeared in more than twenty-five collections, including the following CCAR Press editions: *Mishkan R'fuah: Where Healing Resides* (2012), *L'chol Z'man v'Eit: For Sacred Moments* (2015), *Mishkan HaNefesh: Machzor for the Days of Awe* (2015), *Gates of Shabbat*, revised edition (2016), *Mishkan Aveilut: Where Grief*

Resides (2019), *Mishkan Ga'avah: Where Pride Dwells* (2020); *The Year of Mourning: A Jewish Journey* (2023); and *Prophetic Voices: Renewing and Reimagining Haftarah* (2023). He is a three-time winner of the Peter Lisagor Award for Exemplary Journalism. Alden made *aliyah* to Jerusalem in 2012, where he is Liturgist in Residence at the Pardes Institute of Jewish Studies. He's the founder of ManKind Project Israel. Find his latest works at www.tobendlight.com.

Printed in the USA
CPSIA information can be obtained
at www.ICGtesting.com
CBHW071554090824
12912CB00009B/149